Cracking the Code
A quick reference guide to interpreting patient medical notes

Cracking the Code

A quick reference guide to interpreting patient medical notes

Edited by

Katie Maddock

Cracking the Code: A quick reference guide to interpreting patient medical notes

Edited by Katie Maddock

ISBN: 9781905539-94-9

First published 2015

British Library Cataloguing in Publication Data
A catalogue record for this book is available from the British Library

Notice

Clinical practice and medical knowledge constantly evolve. Standard safety precautions must be followed, but, as knowledge is broadened by research, changes in practice, treatment and drug therapy may become necessary or appropriate. Readers must check the most current product information provided by the manufacturer of each drug to be administered and verify the dosages and correct administration, as well as contraindications. It is the responsibility of the practitioner, utilising the experience and knowledge of the patient, to determine dosages and the best treatment for each individual patient. Any brands mentioned in this book are as examples only and are not endorsed by the publisher. Neither the publisher nor the authors assume any liability for any injury and/or damage to persons or property arising from this publication.

Disclaimer

M&K Publishing cannot accept responsibility for the contents of any linked website or online resource. The existence of a link does not imply any endorsement or recommendation of the organisation or the information or views which may be expressed in any linked website or online resource. We cannot guarantee that these links will operate consistently and we have no control over the availability of linked pages.

To contact M&K Publishing write to:
M&K Update Ltd · The Old Bakery · St. John's Street
Keswick · Cumbria CA12 5AS
Tel: 01768 773030 · Fax: 01768 781099
publishing@mkupdate.co.uk
www.mkupdate.co.uk

Designed and typeset by Mary Blood
Printed in England by McKanes Printers, Keswick

Contents

List of tables

About the contributors

Editor

Katie Maddock PhD, BSc (Hons), PG Dip. Clinical Pharmacy, MAODE (Open), PGCertHE, FHEA, MRPharmS.
Senior Lecturer in Clinical Pharmacy, Keele University

Contributors

Jonathan Berry MPharm, PG Dip. Clinical Pharmacy, PGCertTLHE, MRPharmS, FHEA.
Academic Clinical Educator, School of Pharmacy, Keele University

Val Cartledge BSc (Hons), MSc (Clinical Pharmacy), MRPharmS.
Academic Clinical Educator, School of Pharmacy, Keele University

Marion Cross BPharm (Hons), PG Dip. Clinical Pharmacy, PGCertTLHE, MRPharmS, FHEA.
Academic Clinical Educator, School of Pharmacy, Keele University

Anna Drinkwater BSc (Hons), PG Dip. Clinical Pharmacy, PGCertTLHE, IPresc.
Academic Clinical Educator, School of Pharmacy, Keele University

Kerry Hancock MPharm, PG Dip. Clinical Pharmacy, MRPharmS.
Academic Clinical Educator, School of Pharmacy, Keele University

Jacqui Kinsey MSc, IPresc., MRPharmS, FHEA.
Prescribing Studies Programme Manager, School of Pharmacy, Keele University

Introduction

In the secondary care setting, health professionals, other than doctors, have been actively involved in extracting and interpreting information found within patient medical notes for many years. *Cracking the Code* was originally developed as a tool for use by MPharm students to find their way through the seemingly foreign language of medical notes. It has since been expanded to include explanations of how many common medical examinations and tests are performed and how the results of these should be interpreted.

Cracking the Code covers the basics of the contents of patients' medical notes, from a review of physiological systems to the interpretation of tests and investigations commonly ordered for patients. Common medical terminology used in a review of physiological systems is briefly explained. Commonly encountered investigative procedures are defined and their use explained. Medical laboratory tests are similarly explored.

Much of this book concentrates upon the secondary care environment because this remains the main setting in which healthcare professionals have free and open access to patient medical notes. However the expanding roles of healthcare professionals in the primary care sector, such as pharmacists working within GP practices, and non-medical prescribers in nursing, pharmacy and physiotherapy, mean that all practitioners need to be able to unlock the code. It is hoped that this book will therefore be of use not only to the undergraduate pharmacy students for whom it was originally developed, but also to pre-registration trainees and pharmacists practising in all sectors of the profession, and all other healthcare professionals who access patient medical notes on a routine basis.

This book is not designed to be a comprehensive text to be read from cover to cover. Rather it is a quick reference guide to dip in and out of as required and as the need arises. Many other, larger, texts are available which explain in great detail all of the areas covered in this book, should a deeper exploration be required.

Katie Maddock

Section 1
Medical terminology

In order to interpret a patient's medical notes accurately and with confidence, it is essential to have a good grasp of medical terminology. Some of the terms that are commonly encountered may appear to be very long and complicated but they are generally built up from smaller 'building blocks'. Once the longer terms have been broken down into their constituent blocks, the meaning becomes much clearer.

Medical terms have three basic components: the root, which forms the basis of the word; a prefix – any syllables added in front of the root to modify it and a suffix – any syllables added after the root to modify it. Knowledge of the meanings of a few common roots, prefixes and suffixes enables the understanding of the majority of commonly encountered medical terms.

For example:

(PSEUDO) (HYPO) (PARA) (THYROID) (ISM)
(false) (under) (beside) (thyroid) (condition)
i.e. a condition resembling underactivity of the parathyroid glands.

Tables 1.1 and 1.2, on page 2, contain some of the common roots, prefixes and suffixes that are encountered in clinical practice.

Table 1.1: Common medical prefixes, suffixes and roots

Prefixes		Roots		Suffixes	
a-, an-	without, not	*aden*	relating to glands	*-algia/ -dynia*	pain
brady-	slow	*angi*	blood vessel	*-ia/-iasis/ -ism/-osis*	condition

dys-	defective, abnormal	arth	joint	-itis	inflammation
hyper-	above normal	cardi	heart	-megaly	enlargement
hypo-	below normal	chol	bile/gall bladder	-oma	tumour
iso-	equal	cyt	cell	-pathy	disease, disorder
oli-	few	encephal	brain	-penia	deficiency
peri-	around	enter	intestine	-plasia	formation, development
poly-	many	haem	blood	-plegia	paralysis
tachy-	fast	lapar	abdominal wall	-rrhoea	flowing, discharge
		my	muscle		
		myel	bone marrow or spinal cord		
		neph	kidney		
		ocul	eye		
		ost	bone		
		pan	completely/whole/general		
		pnea	breathing		
		scler	hard/relating to the sclera of the eye		
		ur	urinary system		

Table 1.2: Common surgical suffixes

-centesis	surgical puncture (used for aspiration)
-desis	binding
-ectomy	excision or removal of a body part
-plasty	repair, reconstruction
-rrhapy	surgical suturing
-scopy	use of a viewing instrument
-stomy	creation of an opening
-tomy	the act of cutting, making an incision

Section 2
Patient medical notes

To be involved effectively in the clinical decision-making process, it is important to be able to understand and utilise the information to be found in the patient medical notes. On occasions it is also necessary for the pharmacist to record their interventions in a patient's medical notes.

The medical notes are a chronological record of all significant aspects, including drug treatment, of a patient's care. These are completed for both inpatient stays and for outpatient clinic visits. As a clinical pharmacist you will frequently intervene directly in the care of patients to ensure the safety and efficacy of their treatment. If you do need to intervene in a patient's drug treatment, there are a number of ways in which you can convey this information to the prescriber(s) concerned.

Face to face with the prescriber

This is much the best way to deal with any concerns you have. The modifications you wish to recommend to the prescriber can be discussed and you will all have the information you require to hand. The prescriber is unlikely to document your intervention in the patient's medical notes.

Bleeping or phoning the doctor

If the prescriber is not available for a face to face discussion and the intervention you wish to make is urgent, this is the method used for contacting the prescriber. However, it may not be a convenient time for the prescriber to talk to you. Again, it is unlikely that the prescriber will document your intervention in the patient's medical notes.

Leaving a note on the prescription

This is often used as a method of communication in the hospital environment, particularly if the prescriber is a surgeon, is in theatre and cannot be disturbed. However, such notes are easily lost and if your intervention is not addressed by the prescriber it is difficult to say whether the prescriber saw your note and chose to ignore it, or whether your note was seen at all. Again there is no permanent record of your intervention.

Leaving a message with another member of staff

Your message may not be passed on correctly, if at all. Again there is no permanent record of your intervention.

The following are examples of when you, as a clinical pharmacist, should document your interventions in a patient's medical notes:

- When you recommend that a drug is initiated or discontinued
- When you have discovered that an adverse drug reaction has occurred
- When you discover that the patient is not, or has not been, compliant with their medication
- When your input has been requested by the medical team
- When a critical change to a dosage regimen has occurred
- When an important recommendation has not been followed
- When your written communication would facilitate a review of the patient's drug treatment.

General Layout

The way in which patient medical notes are arranged varies from Trust to Trust. However, the following sections are usually present; it is the order in which they are presented that differs.

Inpatient admissions

The current admission may be found to the front or to the back of this section. All admission notes will contain the same information and previous admissions may be useful for obtaining certain information such as previous drug history (which may not be accurate!).

The current admission usually contains the following information: case history, systems enquiry and examination, differential diagnoses/provisional diagnosis, investigations, drug history, progress.

Outpatient notes

These are often less precise than a full admission, usually consisting of the specific problem, progress since last visit, any relevant measurements and test results, and drug therapy.

Investigations

This section contains, if printed, the clinical chemistry, haematology and microbiology reports, along with the results of X-rays, scans, biopsies, etc.

Letters

Discharge, clinic and referral (from GPs and other consultants) letters will be included.

Other information

This will include copies of previous discharge prescriptions, drug treatment sheets, and nursing notes.

Breakdown of Medical Notes

Case history

The case history is the information obtained from the patient on admission. The process is known as 'clerking' and is usually performed by the on-call doctor (either the Foundation Year 1 (FY1) doctor or the Foundation Year 2 (FY2) doctor) or in some places in pre-admission clinics. A patient may be admitted to hospital via several routes, the most common being: elective (i.e. a planned, booked admission), acute via Accident and Emergency, acute via GP referral or acute self-referral.

Presenting complaint (PC)

These are the main symptoms that have led to the referral and admission to hospital. The PC may also be referred to as 'CC' (chief complaint) or 'C/O' (complains of).

History of presenting complaint (HPC)

This consists of the symptoms experienced in the recent past leading up to the referral, usually with reference to the presenting complaint, as described by the patient. (NB: these headings will not necessarily be used in the patient's medical notes. It is one of the skills required to find this information from the jumble that may be presented.)

Time course

How long has the patient had the symptoms? (E.g. for a few days, months, years.)

Intensity

This is ideally related to everyday activities, known as activities of daily living (ADL). For example:
Shortness of breath (SOB) – the patient can walk to the bus stop and no further.
Pain – usually measured on a score of 1 to 10 (where 1 is little pain and 10 is agony) or by some visual scoring system.

Location

With pain, the patient is asked to point to where it hurts (if the patient is asked to name the place where it hurts, they are likely to use the wrong anatomical terms). Does the pain move (e.g. on bending)?

Setting

What are the circumstances when the symptoms occur? (E.g. after eating, in bed, cold weather.)

Alleviating/aggravating factors

What (if anything) makes the presenting complaint better or worse? (E.g. exercise, eating, drinking alcohol.)

Associated symptoms

Are there any other symptoms that may be related to the presenting complaint? (E.g. a patient with a cough may also have a high temperature.)

Past medical history (PMH)

This should be as full a record as possible of all previous illnesses, accidents or operations.

Childhood illnesses: e.g. chicken pox, measles, rheumatic heart disease, asthma.

Adult illness: this should include both previous illnesses during adulthood and current illnesses (i.e. those that are not the cause of the current admission). Examples include tuberculosis (TB), diabetes type 1 or type 2.

Surgical procedures: e.g. appendectomy, hysterectomy. The position of scars is usually shown on a hexagonal sketch of the abdomen.

Obstetric record: only if relevant (i.e. it should not be present in the notes of a male patient!).

Psychiatric history: This is often unreliable or unobtainable from the patient. To compound the problem, psychiatric notes are usually not kept in the general medical notes and so cannot be referred to. Often, previous medical admission notes will give valuable clues and information.

Drug history (DH)

The history should include: recent and currently prescribed medication, over-the-counter (OTC) medication, other products (e.g. herbal remedies, homeopathic remedies).

This section may be incomplete and/or inaccurate. Unless the patient is very aware, or the referral letter from the GP is very good, or the patient has brought in their own medication, it is often necessary to utilise other resources to obtain the information. Other potentially reliable sources of information about a patient's drug history include: a repeat prescription order form (to be analysed carefully to check the last date upon which each item was previously ordered from the GP), the patient's relatives, direct contact with the patient's GP, the patient's own drugs (PODs), Medication Administration Records (MAR charts) from nursing or residential homes. NICE Clinical Guideline 76 (Medicines adherence: Involving patients in decisions about prescribed medicines and supporting adherence) recommends that those reviewing a patient's medication should enquire about medicines adherence and consider using these sources of information to identify potential non-adherence and whether the patient needs additional support taking their medicines.

It can be useful to refer to previous admissions (if there are any and if they are recent enough) and previous discharge letters and treatment sheets to obtain information about doses, strengths of inhalers, etc.

This section should also include any allergies to drugs that the patient may have (e.g. penicillin, plasters, latex). It is important to distinguish between a true allergic reaction and drug intolerance (i.e. serious side effects) so it is good practice to document the type of reaction such as tongue swelling, rash, nausea.

Social history (SH)

This is the information taken regarding the personal patient details.

Smoking: number per day/pack years. If an ex-smoker, when did the patient stop and how many did they use to smoke? Type smoked – cigarettes, pipe, cigars.

Alcohol (EtOH): recorded as a number of units per week/day, type consumed, how much, when (e.g. socially). This is usually understated by the patient.

Family position: married/single/divorced, how many children.

Occupation: including previous occupation(s) if retired.

Social support: does the patient live alone or with family? Does the patient have a care package in place? What is the patient's ability to self-care?

Family history (FH)

Questions are asked regarding the health of other relatives (mother, father, siblings).

E.g. **Mother** Stroke aged 80

Father MI aged 54

Sister Alive and well (A&W)

Patient examination

Information regarding various body systems is obtained either by questioning the patient or by physical examination, or by a combination of these.

In inpatient notes, the information may consist of a complete body systems review. However, this is not always the case, depending on the situation. Some systems are 'not overtly examined' (NOE). Diagrams are often used to illustrate certain findings, e.g. the position of a wound or an area of pain.

In outpatient notes, the information is likely to be focused on the systems of interest for that particular consultation.

Main methods of examination

Observation

Clinical examination of a patient begins as soon as the medical practitioner sees them. Things that may be obvious upon direct observation of the patient include:

- **Jaundice** – a yellow tinge to the skin and particularly the sclera of the eye
- **Cyanosis** – a blue pallor to the skin (peripheral cyanosis) and/or lips (central cyanosis) due to lack of oxygen in these tissues
- **Oedema** – e.g. puffy ankles
- **Bruising**

- **Smell** – tobacco, cannabis, alcohol, halitosis, acetone (pear drops) on the breath (an indicator of diabetic ketosis)
- **Weight** – underweight or overweight.

Palpation

This is the act of feeling with the hand. Usually it is the application of the fingers with light pressure to the surface of the body in order to detect tenderness; superficial masses and their consistency; position, size and consistency of various organs.

Percussion

This is the act of striking parts of the body with short, sharp (gentle) blows as an aid to diagnosing the condition of the parts beneath by the sounds obtained. The loudness and pitch of the note obtained by percussion give clues as to whether the tissues beneath are solid or infiltrated with either fluid or air. Percussion is most commonly used during examination of the respiratory system.

Percussion is usually performed by placing the palm of the left hand lightly on the skin over the area to be percussed, with the fingers slightly spread. The middle finger is pressed firmly to the skin. The middle joint of the left middle finger is then struck firmly and quickly with the tip of the middle finger of the right hand. The striking finger is removed quickly so that the percussed note is not dampened or dulled.

Auscultation

This is the act of listening for sounds within the body.

This is used to detect respiratory, pleural (chest cavity), cardiac, intestinal, arterial, venous and uterine sounds. It is usually performed with a stethoscope, but may be performed without.

General findings

These include:

- Level of **consciousness**, often given as a Glasgow Coma Scale (GCS) score
- Level of **physical distress**
- **Emotional state**
- **Weight loss** over a given period of time
- **Dehydration**
- **Appetite**
- **Fatigue**
- **Jaundice** – yellow discolouration, first noticeable in the sclera of the eye
- **Anaemia** – patient appears pale – check inside lower eyelid
- **Cyanosis** – Blue discolouration of the skin and mucous membranes. Blue lips indicate central cyanosis. Blue finger tips indicate peripheral cyanosis.
- **Clubbing** – the normal angle between the base of the nail and the nail fold is lost.

Temperature

In a complete body systems review, the temperature of the patient is taken in order to identify either hypo- or hyperthermia. 37° C is the 'normal' oral or ear temperature but this may vary between 35.8° C and 37.2° C (98–99° F). Body temperature also varies over the day and is usually lowest first thing in the morning. A body temperature reading also varies according to where it is measured. Rectal temperature is 0.5° C higher than in the mouth (the axilla is no longer used as it is not a reliable site for measurement). The most favoured site is measurement of temperature at the tympanic membrane using a digital device. This is a reliable and economic way of recording temperature with a high degree of accuracy. Other benefits include low risk of cross infection (if disposable probe covers are used), the insertion technique is easy to perform and perhaps, most importantly, it is well accepted by children.

Fever

Fever (pyrexia) occurs when body temperature is 38° C or higher with hyperpyrexia occurring at 41° C. Fever normally occurs as a response to infection, immunological disturbance or malignancy but rarely may be a response to raised environmental temperatures, particularly if it is humid. Fever may make the patient's skin feel abnormally warm but the patient may feel cool. Conversely a normal skin temperature does not exclude either hypo- or hyperthermia.

A **rigor** is uncontrollable shivering which may occur in response to a rapid increase in body temperature; this may be followed by sweating.

Fever is not a reliable indicator of the seriousness of the disease.

Hypothermia

Hypothermia exists when the patient presents with a core body temperature of less than 35° C and is accompanied by severe shivering with impaired judgement. Hypothermia is easily missed and if suspected, rectal temperature should also be measured. As body temperature falls so do consciousness levels. Coma is common when temperature falls to below 28° C and the patient may appear dead with absent pupillary and tendon reflexes.

Cardiovascular System

Heart rate (HR)

The radial artery pulse is counted for 60 seconds or for 30 seconds and multiplied by 2. In the resting state, the pulse should be between 60 and 90 beats per minute (bpm). Bradycardia in adults is defined as a rate of less than 60 bpm. Tachycardia in adults is defined as a rate of greater than 100 bpm. Paediatric heart rates are summarised in Table 2.1.

Remember that the pulse rate should always be considered in context; a very fit young man may only have a pulse rate of 45 bpm, whilst a pulse rate of 65 bpm in a patient with heart failure may be considered to be bradycardic.

The rhythm of the heartbeat is also checked using one of the larger pulses (carotid, femoral or brachial). The rhythm is classed as regular or irregular. An irregular pulse may be regularly irregular (ectopic beats or second degree AV block) or irregularly irregular (most commonly due to atrial fibrillation). If it is irregular, it is checked by auscultation with a stethoscope.

Table 2.1: Normal paediatric heart rates

Age	Heart rate at rest (bpm)
< 1 year	110–160
1 to 2 years	100–150
2 to 5 years	95–140
5 to 12 years	80–120
> 12 years	60–100

Blood pressure (BP)

The definition of normal BP is open to debate. It can be assumed that normal values are as shown:

Systolic = 100–140 mmHg
Diastolic = 60–90 mmHg

The conditions under which blood pressure is measured are key, as they may influence the result obtained. Patients who are stressed, excited, too warm or too cold may give abnormal readings. According to NICE Clinical Guideline 127 (Clinical management of primary hypertension in adults), patients should be quiet and seated in a relaxed, temperate environment before a reading is taken. A diagnosis of hypertension, following a clinic BP measurement of > 140/90 mmHg, should be confirmed using ambulatory blood pressure monitoring (APBM) where possible. It should be noted that NICE CG127 states that there is a lower threshold for a confirmation of a diagnosis of hypertension (≥ 135/85 mmHg) if ABPM or home blood pressure monitoring (HBPM) is used.

To check for postural hypotension, a reading is taken with the patient either seated or supine (lying down), followed by a second reading taken after the patient has been standing for at least one minute.

Heart – apex beat (AB)

The apex beat is the result of the part of the left ventricle furthest away from the centre of the heart striking the chest wall during systole. It can be palpated by following the mid-clavicular (middle of the collarbone) line down to the 4th or 5th intercostal space (between the 4th and 5th ribs) on the left side of the chest. It will normally lift the fingers during palpation. The apex beat may be difficult to find in patients who are overweight or very muscular. In patients who have conditions which may cause hyperinflation of the lungs (e.g. asthma or emphysema) it can also be difficult to find.

Certain conditions, such as left ventricular hypertrophy, may cause a 'heave' which lifts the hand rather than just the fingers upon palpation. Following a myocardial infarction, the apex beat may be felt in a different position. Other conditions which may cause a displaced apex beat include: cardiomegaly, pleural effusion, tension pneumothorax, chest wall deformities. In very rare cases of dextrocardia (where the heart is either shifted to the right in the torso, or is a mirror of a normal heart), the apex beat may be felt on the right-hand side of the chest.

A 'thrill' is a vibration that can be felt in the chest wall when palpating with the palm of the hand. This is caused by the turbulent movement of blood over or through a heart valve.

Heart sounds

These are listened for using a stethoscope using either the diaphragm or the bell. Certain regions of the chest wall are preferred for certain sounds, but all sounds can be heard.

The first two heart sounds are normally described as 'lub dub, lub dub'.

S1 = 1st heart sound – *lub*

This is a low-pitched, long sound due to closure of the mitral and tricuspid valves at the beginning of systole.

S2 = 2nd heart sound – *dub*

This is a high-pitched, relatively rapid snap due to the closure of the semilunar valves at the end of ventricular systole.

The next two heart sounds are unusual.

S3 = 3rd heart sound

This is normal in children and adolescents, but abnormal in adults. It resembles water running into a sack. It is due to rapid ventricular filling after the mitral and tricuspid valves open.

S4 = 4th heart sound

Heard in patients with hypertension and older adults, this is a very low-pitched sound and is rarely heard. If it is to be heard, it occurs just before S1 and is caused by atrial contraction against a stiff ventricle. Left ventricular hypertrophy is a common cause.

Murmurs

Heart murmurs are other heart sounds associated with turbulent blood flow. Although they are abnormal, they are often present and are not always clinically significant as they don't always cause symptoms.

Jugular venous pressure (JVP)

This is a measure of the severity of right-sided heart failure or of fluid overload. The measurement is taken by propping the patient at an angle of 45° and viewing the point of pulsation of the internal jugular vein in the neck on the patient's right side, with the head tilted slightly to the left. The JVP is measured as the vertical height in centimetres from the top of the jugular pulsation to the sternal angle. The sternal angle is where the sternum and the manubrium meet at the second rib.

In patients with normal cardiac pathology, the JVP may not be seen. If it is visible it should be less than 3 cm. In a patient's notes, the JVP is recorded as the number of centimetres raised above normal or by a number of arrows.

E.g. JVP raised 2 cm *or* JVP↑↑

Chest pain

Chest pain as a result of cardiac ischaemia is often described as tightness in the middle of the chest, a crushing, vice-like pain or as a band around the chest.

It is often accompanied by sweating, nausea and a discomfort in the arms (particularly the left) and in the wrists and hands. The pain may also be referred to the jaw, the neck and between the shoulder blades (intrascapular pain).

Dyspnoea (breathlessness)

Cardiac conditions which may present with dyspnoea as a symptom include angina, heart failure, pulmonary hypertension and pulmonary embolism.

In heart failure, the degree of dyspnoea a patient experiences is used in the New York Heart Association classification of heart failure. Initially, the patient may be only short of breath on exertion (SOBOE), e.g. when climbing stairs or walking. In later stages of heart failure, the patient may be permanently short of breath (SOB).

Orthopnoea (paroxysmal nocturnal dyspnoea – PND)

This is where fluid accumulates in the lungs when the patient is lying down. The patient needs to sit up for relief, gasping for breath and will often open a window to 'get more air'. This is a very frightening experience for the patient and has been described as 'drowning from the inside'.

It is eased by the patient propping themselves up to sleep and the number of pillows used by the patient is a rough guide to the severity of the condition, e.g. the patient may be described as suffering from '3 pillow orthopnoea'. Some patients may even have to sleep in a chair.

Orthopnoea is diagnostic of severe left ventricular failure (LVF).

Oedema

Heart failure and other medical conditions can result in the accumulation of fluid in soft tissues. The location of this fluid depends on gravity. Therefore a mobile patient is likely to have swollen ankles and feet, whilst a bed-bound patient will have sacral oedema (oedema at the base of the spine). In heart failure the oedema is usually bilateral. Generally if the JVP is normal then the oedema has a non-cardiac cause. This oedema is described as pitting oedema – putting pressure on the area will leave an indentation that will remain for a long while.

Patients with cardiac failure can also present with pulmonary oedema.

Respiratory System

Inspection

The shape of the chest is inspected and recorded – for example, barrel chest (chronic obstructive pulmonary disease) or pigeon chest (chronic childhood asthma).

Symmetry is recorded – does the chest expand symmetrically? If not, the pathology is on the restricted side.

Respiratory effort is recorded. For example, the use of accessory muscles of respiration is indicative of severe acute asthma.

During the respiratory examination, there are other signs of respiratory disease that should be noted. These include:

Cyanosis – sign of:	Fingernail clubbing – sign of:	Haemoptysis (blood in sputum) – sign of:
Pulmonary embolism Worsening COPD Worsening asthma Pneumonia Bronchiectasis	Severe lung infections (e.g. tuberculosis) Cystic fibrosis Lung cancer Empyema (a collection of pus within an existing lesion within the lungs)	Tuberculosis Acute bronchitis Chronic bronchitis Pneumonia Bronchiectasis Lung cancer

Nicotine staining of the fingers is also a useful diagnostic sign.

Palpation

The position of the mediastinum (the organs within the centre of the chest including the heart, major blood vessels, trachea and the oesophagus) is diagnostic of several lung conditions. The patient should be observed from the front for any obvious deviation of the trachea. The trachea is gently palpated by placing the tip of an index finger in the suprasternal notch (the bony notch at the base of the throat). This is a very uncomfortable procedure and so minimum pressure should be used. The trachea is often slightly deviated to the right in healthy patients. A major shift in the position of the trachea indicates a major shift in the position of the upper mediastinum. This can be caused by upper lobe fibrosis, upper lobe collapse, lung cancer (the mass of the tumour displaces the mediastinum), a tension pneumothorax or a massive pleural effusion.

Percussion

The left middle finger is placed firmly on the chest wall and is firmly tapped with the right middle finger. This is done over all lung fields. Both lungs are usually equal in resonance. The terms used to describe the results of percussion of the chest are summarised in Table 2.2 (see page 14).

Table 2.2: Terms used to describe lung sounds upon percussion

Term	Description
Resonant	Normal lung
Hyperresonant	Lower in pitch: air-filled space (pneumothorax)
Dull	Higher in pitch and indicative of solid tissue (consolidation due to pneumonia, collapse)
Stony dull	Fluid (effusion)

Auscultation

Listening to sounds over the lung fields using a stethoscope bell as the sounds are of low frequency. The sounds listened to are whilst talking or whispering (vocal sounds) or breathing (breath sounds). In a patient's notes, the terms used for breath and vocal sounds are:

- **Normal**
- **Diminished**
- **Absent**
- **Increased**

Breath sounds

Normal breath sounds are vesicular (rustling). The intensity of the sounds heard depends very much on the tissue through which the sound is transmitted. In normal lungs the breath sounds are decreased because parenchymal tissue transmits sounds poorly.

Breath sounds are often diminished in patients with a pneumothorax, pleural effusion, obstruction of a major bronchus (due to cancer or a collapsed lung) or who are obese. Occasionally breath sounds may be diminished due to the presence of secretions. In this latter case, asking the patient to cough may clear the lungs slightly and make the sounds more audible.

Vocal sounds

Healthy lungs transmit low-pitched speech and knock out high-pitched sounds so that whispered speech is not heard. If consolidated lung is present (pneumonia) the normal speech sounds are heard and the consolidation amplifies whispered speech so this is heard too. Normal speech is muffled where there is fluid present or if there is a collapse of lung tissue.

Sonorous sounds such as 'ninety-nine' cause vibration on the chest wall in healthy lungs. They are less well heard or felt in consolidated lung tissue and obliterated if pleural fluid is present. *Aegophony* is where an 'eee' sound is changed to 'aaa' if a solid or liquid mass is present.

Added sounds

Wheezes (rhonchi) are continuous musical sounds caused by obstruction or narrowing of the airways, particularly on expiration. They are often the result of airway narrowing and are usually heard in patients with asthma, chronic bronchitis and emphysema.

Crackles (crepitations) are interrupted, non-musical sounds caused by the collapse of peripheral airways on expiration. They are generally fine and high-pitched if heard at the bottom of the lungs (distally), usually due to pulmonary oedema. They are generally coarse and low-pitched if heard proximally (towards the middle of the lungs) and indicate a respiratory tract infection. Crackles are considered to be clinically insignificant if they disappear on coughing.

Rubs are well-localised creakings or groanings which sound like leather creaking or someone walking on very fresh snow. Rubs are heard when there is inflammation of the pleural membranes (pleurisy), which then rub over each other. They are often associated with pleural pain and are a symptom of pneumonia or pulmonary embolism.

Respiratory rate

This is determined by counting the number of times the chest rises and falls.

A normal adult respiratory rate is between 10 and 16 breaths per minute. Tachypnoea is defined as a respiratory rate of greater than 20 breaths per minute.

Paediatric respiratory rates are summarised in Table 2.3.

Table 2.3: Normal paediatric respiratory rates

Age (years)	Respiratory rate (breaths per minute)
< 1 year	30–40
1 to 2 years	25–35
2 to 5 years	25–30
5 to 12 years	20–25
> 12 years	15–20

Cheyne-Stokes respiration

This is where the breathing becomes progressively deeper, then shallower, in cycles. There may be periods where the patient stops breathing (apnoea). It is caused by brainstem lesions or compression, e.g. stroke, tumour or raised intracranial pressure due to trauma. It may also be caused by a prolonged lung-brain circulation time, e.g. in chronic pulmonary oedema or poor cardiac output. It often signifies a poor prognosis.

Sputum

In a patient's notes this is described by the amount (often signified by a number of '+' signs, e.g. +++) and the colour. The colour of sputum can be a useful diagnostic tool for any underlying respiratory condition. Healthy patients produce little sputum but that which is produced is clear.

Patients who produce quantities of clear, watery and/or frothy sputum may be suffering from pulmonary oedema, although it may also be indicative of lung cancer. Occasionally the sputum may be pink in colour.

Patients with asthma or chronic bronchitis usually present with sputum that is similar to mucus in consistency and which is clear, white or grey in colour. Sputum in acute viral respiratory infections is similar in colour and consistency. Purulent sputum, indicative of bacterial bronchopulmonary infections, is usually yellow, green or brown in colour. Patients with asthma may produce sputum rich in eosinophils which appears similar in colour and consistency to brown mucopurulent sputum.

Sputum with the presence of blood (haemoptysis) is diagnostic for bronchial carcinoma, tuberculosis (both conditions present with large amounts of blood in the sputum) or pneumonia (traces of blood).

Cough

Cough is a relatively non-specific symptom of respiratory conditions as a cough is a reaction to irritation anywhere from the pharynx to the lungs. The cough's duration can be useful to know, as can the time of day it is most prevalent. A cough first thing in the morning is symptomatic of post-nasal drop due to rhinosinusitis. A cough on lying down suggests gastro-oesophageal reflux disease. Worsening asthma may present as a persistent night-time cough.

Pleural effusion

This is an escape of fluid into the pleural cavity. The fluid is tapped and analysed to distinguish between an exudate and a transudate. Exudate contains a high concentration of protein, cells and other materials. This has escaped from the blood into tissues and is often due to pneumonia, carcinoma or pulmonary tuberculosis. Transudate has a low content of protein, cells and solid materials. It is of tissue origin with a high fluidity and may be due to cardiac failure or cirrhosis.

Other terms used

Empyema is a collection of pus in the pleural space resulting from a lung infection. This fluid may be up to 500 mL in volume and it exerts pressure on the lungs which results in shortness of breath and chest pain amongst other symptoms.

Stridor is defined as noisy breathing due to an obstruction within the larynx or the lungs. It is a harsh, high-pitched sound and the cause should be investigated as a matter of urgency. Common causes of stridor include inhalation of a foreign object, swelling of the throat or upper airways and spasm of the vocal cords or muscles of the upper airways.

Pulse oximetry

This measures arterial oxygen saturation (SpO_2) by determining the differential absorption of light by oxyhaemoglobin and deoxyhaemoglobin. In acutely ill patients with no risk of CO_2 retention, SpO_2 should be maintained at 94–98%.

Arterial blood gases

Arterial blood gases (ABGs) – PaO_2 and $PaCO_2$ – and acid-base (pH) status determine whether the patient has any disturbances in acid-base balance as shown in Table 2.4.

Typical normal ranges when breathing air at sea level are:

pH   7.35–7.45
PaO_2 11–13 kPa
$PaCO_2$ 4.7–6.0 kPa
HCO_3^- 24.0–30.0 mmol/L

Table 2.4: Summary of arterial blood gas results

Disturbance	pH	CO2	HCO3	Some causes
Respiratory acidosis	low	high	high	severe acute asthma, severe pneumonia, exacerbation COPD
Respiratory alkalosis	high	low	low	hyperventilation due to anxiety/panic, CNS causes
Metabolic acidosis	low	low	low	DKA, poisoning, AKI, Addison's disease
Metabolic alkalosis	high	high	high	severe vomiting, loss of potassium

CURB-65 and CRB-65 scores

Assessment of the severity of community-acquired pneumonia can be undertaken using the CURB-65 score in the hospital setting and the CRB-65 score in the community setting. To obtain the CURB-65 score, one point is awarded for any of the following:

- Confusion*
- Urea > 7 mmol/L
- Respiratory rate ≥ 30 resps/min
- Blood pressure (SBP < 90 mmHg or DBP ≤ 60 mmHg)
- Age ≥ 65 years

*Defined as a Mental Test Score of 8 or less, or a new disorientation in person, time or place.

The CRB-65 score is calculated as the CURB-65 score, but omitting the urea measurement. Table 2.5 summarises the implications for the patient of the CURB-65/CRB-65 score.

Table 2.5: CURB-65 and CRB-65 scores

CURB-65 (hospital)		CRB-65 (community)	
Score	Mortality	Score	Mortality
0 or 1	Low	0	Low
2	Intermediate	1 or 2	Intermediate
3 or more	High	3 or 4	High

17

Gastrointestinal System (GIT)

Before any physical examination is made, a patient will be asked about their appetite, any nausea or vomiting, frequency of bowel movements, stool appearance, any pain (including non-abdominal pain), the presence of heartburn, dyspepsia or flatulence. A record will be made of any visible signs of jaundice, clubbing of fingers or other physical signs of liver disease. The patient's height, weight and waist circumference will be recorded along with an estimate of their body mass index (BMI). It should be remembered that the BMI is only an estimation of obesity and may over- or underestimate adiposity. For example, the BMI tends to overestimate adiposity in athletes.

Physical examination of the abdomen

The abdomen is palpated with the patient supine and their head resting on one or two pillows only. This allows the abdominal muscles to relax, enabling the structures underneath to be felt. Palpation of the abdomen is mapped as in the abdominal diagram (Figure 1). The abdomen may also be considered in terms of quadrants: right upper quadrant (RUQ), right lower quadrant (RLQ), left upper quadrant (LUQ), left lower quadrant (LLQ).

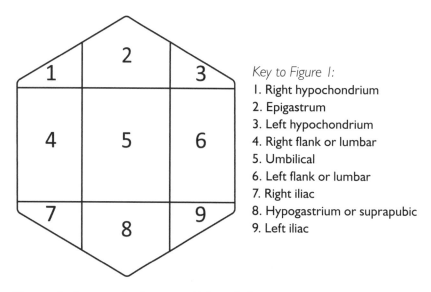

Key to Figure 1:
1. Right hypochondrium
2. Epigastrum
3. Left hypochondrium
4. Right flank or lumbar
5. Umbilical
6. Left flank or lumbar
7. Right iliac
8. Hypogastrium or suprapubic
9. Left iliac

Figure 1: Anatomical areas of the abdomen

Abdominal discomfort upon palpation is described as guarding or tenderness. Guarding is the protection of the viscera by the abdominal muscles. This may be voluntary (where the patient tenses the muscles in anticipation of discomfort) or involuntary. Involuntary guarding is indicative of inflammation of the parietal peritoneum. In extreme cases, the abdominal muscles show rigidity.

When the abdomen is compressed with fingers, any pain or discomfort felt by the patient may be worsened on withdrawal of the hand, possibly away from the site palpated. This is known as rebound tenderness and implies inflammation of the structures beneath. The site of any tenderness is suggestive of underlying medical conditions. For example, tenderness in the epigastrum suggests peptic ulcer disease, whilst right iliac fossal tenderness may be appendicitis or Crohn's disease.

Liver and spleen

Normally, the liver cannot be palpated below the ribcage. If the liver is enlarged (hepatomegaly), it may be palpated whilst the patient inhales deeply. A record is made of the number of centimetres below the costal margin (the edge of the ribcage). It may also be expressed in terms of fingerbreadths. The spleen is only palpable if enlarged.

Bowel sounds

These are determined by listening with the diaphragm of a stethoscope placed to the right of the umbilicus. Bowel sounds are the gurgling noises produced by normal peristalsis of the gut. They are only recorded as being absent after two minutes of listening. Absent bowel sounds indicate either paralytic ileus or peritonitis.

Normal bowel sounds usually occur every 5 to 10 seconds, but this is only a guide. Bowel sounds which occur more frequently than this are a symptom of intestinal obstruction or Crohn's disease.

Other terms commonly used in recording the results of examination of the GI tract are summarised in Table 2.6.

Table 2.6: Common terms used following examination of the GI tract

Term	Description
Ascites	Fluid in the abdominal cavity. E.g. liver failure, liver metastases
Coffee-ground vomit	Vomit containing partially digested blood. E.g. gastro-intestinal bleed
Dysphagia	Difficulty in swallowing. E.g. oesophageal carcinoma
Haematemesis	Vomiting blood. E.g. liver failure, peptic ulceration
Malaena	Blood in faeces

Nervous System

This is not always examined in detail, depending upon the differential diagnoses under consideration. The patient may be asked about the following: parasthesia (pins and needles), 'funny turns' or faints, headache, changes in speech or coordination, changes in memory or ability to concentrate. A patient's relatives or carers may also provide valuable information on these latter two items, along with any personality changes.

Cranial nerve testing

The cranial nerves, their function and the tests used in their examination are described in Table 2.7.

Table 2.7: The cranial nerves, their functions and routine tests

Cranial nerve	Function	Test
Olfactory (I)	Sense of smell	Test with a common substance, e.g. soap. This is of limited clinical value and so is rarely tested.
Optic (II)	Visual acuity	Snellen chart. Only tested if a problem with visual acuity is suspected.
Ocular (III), trochlear (IV), abducens (VI)	Eye movement and pupil size	The patient is asked to follow the movement of the examiner's finger. Non-parallel movements of the eyes indicate an underlying problem.
Trigeminal (V)	Sensation to the mouth and face; motor control of the muscles of mastication	Light touch to the face, superficial pain response, nasal tickle. Observation of wasting of the muscles of mastication. Corneal reflex and jaw jerk.
Facial (VII)	Control of facial expression. Taste from the anterior two-thirds of the tongue	Inspection for facial asymmetry (e.g. raising eyebrows), spontaneous or involuntary movements. Power is tested by asking the patient to blow out their cheeks against pressure.
Vestibulocochlear (VIII)	Hearing	Whispered voice and/or tuning fork tests (Weber's and Rinne's tests).
Glossopharyngeal (IX), vagus (X)	Swallowing, articulation of speech, sensation from the pharynx and larynx	Speech is checked for difficulty in speaking (dysarthria) or difficulty in producing vocal sounds (dysphonia). Movement of the palate and uvula are checked by asking the patient to say 'Ah'.
Accessory (XI)	Shoulder shrugging, turning and flexing of the head	Trapezoid and sternocleidomastoid muscles are visually inspected for wasting and/or asymmetry. Power is checked by asking the patient to shrug their shoulders against downward pressure from the examiner and to turn the head against sideways pressure.
Hypoglossal (XII)	Tongue movements	Visual inspection for unilateral tongue wasting. Speed of movement of tongue flicking from side to side (slowness is an abnormal finding).

Reflexes

Deep tendon reflexes

These form part of the motor function assessment, together with muscle strength assessment. Deep tendon reflexes are involuntary contractions of muscles in response to stretch. In medical testing, the stretch is induced by a controlled blow with a rubber tendon hammer striking briskly against a tendon or muscle sheath.

Examples of tendon reflexes tested include:

- biceps reflex
- triceps reflex
- knee jerk
- ankle jerk.

Tendon reflexes are graded as absent, diminished, normal or increased.

Plantar reflexes

Plantar reflexes are tested by stroking the outer edge of the sole of the foot towards the little toe with a blunt instrument. The normal response is a downward movement of the big toe and the foot (down-going plantar reflex). An abnormal response – a Babinski response – is when the big toe and foot extend upwards (up-going plantar reflex).

Coordination

Checks on a patient's coordination are performed when there is suspicion of cerebellar damage or disease. Examples of coordination tests include: finger-to-nose (the patient has to touch the examiner's finger and their own nose alternately with each hand), heel-to-shin (the patient rubs the heel of one leg against the shin of the other and should be able to retain the heel on the shin), gait (the patient's usual gait is observed for co-ordination, symmetry, fluidity and balance).

Sensory examination

A sensory (or neurological) examination is a systematic examination of the function of the nerves which transmit sensory information to the brain such as touch, pain, joint position, temperature, vibration. This is rarely done unless the patient specifically mentions any sensory symptoms or if any underlying sensory pathology is suspected such as spinal cord damage.

Glasgow Coma Scale

The Glasgow Coma Scale (GCS) is a neurological scale developed to standardise the monitoring of patients with potential or established neurological damage and is a measure of consciousness level. It is used in both emergency situations where there is potentially either medical or traumatic brain injury and on intensive care units. The GCS is recorded as a score between 3 (deeply unconscious) and 15. Three parameters are examined as shown in Table 2.8 (see page 22). A GCS of $\leq$ 8 indicates severe brain injury; 9 to 12, moderate brain injury; $\geq$ 13, mild or no brain injury.

Table 2.8: The Glasgow Coma Scale

| Score | Best response | | |
	Eye	Verbal	Motor
1	No eye opening	No verbal response	No motor response
2	Eyes open to pain	Incomprehensible sounds	Extension to pain
3	Eyes open to verbal command	Inappropriate words	Flexion to pain
4	Eyes open spontaneously	Confused	Withdrawal from pain
5	–	Orientated	Localising pain
6	–	–	Obeys commands

Mental state

Mental state is assessed as the orientation of the patient in terms of person, time and place.

If the patient appears to be confused, a further test may be conducted to assess their mental capacity. There are various tools available to do this and the most commonly used is the Mini Mental State Examination (MMSE). The MMSE consists of a series of questions and tests, each of which scores points if answered correctly. If every answer is correct, a maximum score of 30 points is possible. The MMSE tests a number of different mental abilities, including a person's memory, attention and language.

The MMSE contains a range of different questions and tests. Below are four sample questions that give an indication of the style of the MMSE.

1 Orientation to time
'What is the date?'

2 Registration
'Listen carefully. I am going to say three words. You say them back after I stop. Ready? Here they are... apple [pause], penny [pause], table [pause]. Now repeat those words back to me.'
[Repeat up to 5 times, but score only the first trial.]

3 Naming
'What is this?' [Point to a pencil or pen.]

4 Reading
'Please read this and do what it says.' [Show examinee the following words on the stimulus form: Close your eyes.]

Skin

Observation

This should be a description of the appearance of the skin, including the shape and distribution of any lesions present. A symmetrical or universal skin eruption is suggestive of a systemic cause. An asymmetrical rash that appears to have spread from a single point of origin is usually indicative of a bacterial, fungal or viral infection. Patients are also asked about the time of onset of any skin symptoms, any possible provoking factors (e.g. a change of detergent), the presence of itch and any other symptoms (which may be non-skin symptoms).

Some common terms used to describe skin lesions or the appearance of the skin are outlined in Table 2.9.

Table 2.9: Common terms used to describe skin conditions

Term	Description
Bulla	Fluid-filled blister, more than 5 to 10 mm in diameter
Erythema	Redness
Exfoliative	Flaking off
Fissure	Crack in the epidermis
Indurated	Thick, hardened
Macule	Flat spot, up to 1 cm in diameter
Maculopapular	Eruption of macules and papules
Nodule	Solid lesion > 1 cm in diameter
Papule	Raised spot up to 1 cm in diameter
Petechia	Pin-point purplish-red spot under the skin
Purpura	Small haemorrhage under the skin or mucous membrane
Pustule	Pus-containing blister
Vesicle	Fluid-filled blister up to 5 to 10 mm in diameter

Musculoskeletal System

At the beginning of the examination, patients will be asked about any pain or stiffness. The origin of the pain – joints (arthralgia), muscle (myalgia) or other soft tissues should be established. The location of the pain and the number of joints involved (if any) are suggestive of the diagnosis. For example, extreme pain in the base joint of the big toe is suggestive of gout.

The nature of any pain experienced by the patient is also explored. Muscle pain is usually described as stiffness and deep pain that is made worse by use of the affected muscles. Bone pain is often described as deep or boring, whilst the pain of a fracture is sharp and stabbing and relieved by splinting and rest of the affected bone. Shooting pain is most likely caused by a mechanical impingement of a peripheral nerve or nerve root. A very common example of this is the shooting pain of sciatica, which appears to originate in the buttock and may shoot down the back of the leg. The cause is usually protrusion of a lumbar disc impinging on the sciatic nerve root.

If a patient is experiencing joint pain, the number of joints involved, their location and the pattern of distribution of pain are often diagnostic. For example, rheumatoid arthritis presents as a symmetrical inflammation of both small and large joints in the arms, hands, shoulders, hips, knees and feet. The patient will also be asked about the duration of their symptoms and whether the pain and/or stiffness is relieved on movement or after rest.

The degree of swelling around a joint and the time it took to develop are also diagnostic. All inflamed or infected joints will be warm to the touch. Acute injury to bones or ligaments which results in bleeding into a joint will produce swelling within minutes. Swelling in response to acute injury to cartilage, which is non-vascular in nature, will take much longer (hours or days) to develop.

Other symptoms which are non-musculoskeletal in origin should also be asked about; fever, rashes, malaise, weight loss can all be associated with musculoskeletal conditions. Some drugs, such as statins, may also cause muscle or joint pain so a full drug history is essential.

Once a history of symptoms has been taken, a physical examination will take place with the aim of causing the patient as little extra pain or discomfort as possible. Joints are tested for warmth, swelling, stability and deformity. The range of movement will be measured and, where only one side of the body is affected, compared to the normal side.

Section 3
Investigative procedures

Definition of Procedures

Radiography

X-rays are a form of electromagnetic radiation with wavelengths of between 0.01 and 10 nanometres. For medical diagnostic imaging purposes they are generated in a vacuum tube by firing a beam of electrons onto a copper anode. The collision of the electrons with the anode generates energy, 99% of which is released as heat. The remaining 1% of energy is released as X-rays. In medical imaging, the area of the human body to be imaged is subjected to a targeted beam of X-rays which are captured either on sensitised photographic film or, more commonly, by a digital detector. A shadow image is produced which is known as a radiograph or 'plain' X-ray. There are considered to be four basic densities in radiography. The most radiopaque structures within the human body are calcified (e.g. bones and teeth) and absorb X-rays, producing a white image on the radiograph. Soft tissue structures (e.g. the heart) absorb fewer X-rays and so they appear more grey in colour; fatty tissues produce a slightly darker image than this. Radiolucent structures (such as those containing air) absorb few X-rays and will produce a dark image on the radiograph.

Computed tomography

Computed tomography (CT scanning) is another imaging technique that utilises X-rays. In this case, the X-ray tube and detectors move around the patient on a single axis of rotation. The patient is supine and the gantry, which contains the X-ray tube and detectors, is placed around the part of the body to be scanned. The data produced is fed through a computer algorithm, resulting in a series of images, or slices, through the body. CT scans produce much higher-resolution images than plain radiographs in terms of the differences in radiopacity observed. It is also possible for the computer program to construct a three-dimensional image from the two-dimensional slices produced by the scanner.

Contrast media

Contrast media are used to enhance the radiopacity of structures in the body. For example, barium is used to outline the gastrointestinal tract on plain X-rays, whilst iodine-based intravenous media are used to enhance blood vessels in angiography and the urinary system in urography.

Positron emission tomography

Positron emission tomography (PET scanning) uses positron-emitting isotopes of common biologically important elements such as oxygen or carbon. These isotopes have a short half-life and emit two gamma-rays as they decay. The gamma-rays are detected by a gamma camera and the resulting image shows the distribution of the isotope throughout the body. A gamma camera consists of a large sodium iodide crystal which, when struck and activated by gamma-rays, emits light. The light is amplified within the camera and converted to an electronic pulse which is, in turn, amplified by a processing unit.

This technique is often used to image physiological processes such as the metabolism of glucose. The most commonly used agent in PET scanning is F-18 fluorodeoxyglucose (FDG). This analogue of glucose is used to identify the uptake of glucose into cells following glucose metabolism. In a healthy human, the areas of concentration of FDG should be the brain (high uptake), the kidneys and the bladder (excretion). In cancer, tumour deposits often have a high uptake of glucose and so an abnormal distribution of FDG will be observed on the image. FDG can also be used to stage solid cancers such as lung cancer.

Radionuclide imaging

An ideal diagnostic radionuclide is one which emits gamma-rays and has a radioactive half-life of sufficient length for preparation, transportation, administration and imaging, but short enough to prevent unnecessary radiation remaining in the body. It should also be readily available and easy to formulate into different preparations for uptake into different body tissues. Technetium-99m (^{99m}Tc) best meets these properties. It is generated from the decay of molybdenum-99 (^{99}Mo). As ^{99m}Tc decays to the more stable isotope ^{99}Tc, it emits a gamma-ray which is detected by a gamma camera for imaging purposes.

Magnetic resonance imaging (MRI)

MRI scanners utilise the magnetic properties of hydrogen nuclei in the body (i.e. protons). The majority of hydrogen in the human body is found as part of water molecules. In a state of equilibrium, these protons spin in all directions. When placed within a magnetic field at the appropriate resonance frequency, they are induced to spin in the same direction. The pulse of magnetism is removed and the protons then return to their equilibrium state. As they do so, they release a characteristic radiofrequency (RF) signal which is picked up by a number of RF receivers built into the scanner. The protons in different tissues return to their equilibrium state at different rates and this information determines the contrast between tissue types. Bone gives off no signal and so does not produce an image on an MRI scan.

Gradient coils within the scanner apply different magnetic fields in different positions and so control the orientation of the image produced. These coils are switched on and off rapidly and produce the characteristic noise of an MRI scanner for which patients are usually provided ear plugs.

The magnet strength of an MRI scanner is measured in teslas (T). Most clinical scanners are fitted with 1.5 T superconductor magnets cooled with liquid helium; scanners are available from 0.5 T to 7 T.

Before a patient can undergo an MRI, they must be reviewed to exclude any items that may be ferromagnetic, electrically conductive or RF reactive. Such items may be extremely dangerous to the patient, the equipment or other people in the scanner room if placed in an MRI scanner. The (not exhaustive) list of potential problem items includes:

- Permanent pacemakers
- Cochlear implants
- Surgical clips
- Artificial heart valves
- Implanted drug infusion ports
- Artificial limbs
- Metallic joints
- Implanted nerve stimulators
- Surgical staples, stents, pins, screws or plates
- Metal fragments embedded in the body or the eye (e.g. shrapnel, swarf from metalworking).

Titanium and titanium alloys are considered safe within an MRI scanner.

Medical devices included in the list above are categorised as either MR-Safe (non-magnetic, non-electronically conducting, non-RF responsive), MR-Conditional (tested and shown to be safe within certain magnetic field strengths) or MR-Unsafe (significantly ferromagnetic).

Before an MRI scan, patients are usually required to change into a hospital gown to avoid any unexpected metallic items in their clothing causing problems in the scanner. They are also asked to remove any jewellery (except wedding rings). Items such as mobile phones and wallets should be left outside the scanner room as the high levels of magnetism may damage bank cards and mobile phones.

Ultrasonography

Ultrasonography is the visualisation of soft tissues by the use of very high-frequency sound. The sound is directed into the body from a transducer on the skin; acoustic contact between the transducer and the skin is improved by the use of an aqueous gel. Ultrasound imaging is not of any great use in the examination of the lungs or bone, as air and calcified tissues absorb the larger part of the ultrasound beam.

Ultrasound is very useful for imaging fluid-filled structures in the body such as the bladder, the gall bladder, the amniotic sac in pregnant women, and cysts. Fluid-filled structures will produce an echo from their walls but no echo from the fluid within. Calcified, solid structures will absorb the ultrasound. Hence the gall bladder can be imaged and any gall stones within will show up as shadow.

Ultrasound techniques can also be used to image blood flow through the heart or blood vessels by exploiting the Doppler effect. When blood flows towards the transducer, the reflected sound is at a higher frequency than that transmitted. The opposite applies when blood flows away from the transducer. This difference in frequencies is known as the Doppler shift. A coloured image is superimposed onto the standard image, with blood flow towards the transducer coloured red and blood flow away from the transducer coloured blue. Doppler studies are used in the diagnosis of venous thrombosis and arterial stenosis along with the measurement of tumour blood flow and foetal blood flow through the umbilical artery.

Endoscopy

Endoscopy is the technique of examining the interior of the body by inserting a camera (endoscope) directly into the cavity to be examined. Rigid or flexible fibre-optic endoscopes are used and the image is either viewed directly through an eyepiece or transmitted to a screen.

Endoscopy is most commonly used to examine the gastrointestinal tract, the respiratory tract, the ear and the genitourinary tract. It can also be used, through incisions in the skin, to examine the pelvic cavity, the abdominal cavity, the interior of the chest and the interior of joints. The tip of the endoscope can be changed according to the procedure it is being used for.

The patient does not generally require a general anaesthetic for endoscopic procedures. Patients who are undergoing examination of the GI or respiratory systems are usually sedated with a short-acting benzodiazepine such as midazolam.

Electrography

Electrography is the graphical recording of changes in electrical potential. The two most commonly encountered procedures are the electrocardiogram (ECG) and the electroencephalogram (EEG).

An ECG is used to monitor and record the electrical conduction system of the heart. Electrodes are attached to the skin of the chest. These detect the electrical impulses generated when cardiac muscle cells polarise and depolarise. The image (trace) produced measures both the rhythm and rate of the heartbeat and gives an indication of any cardiac damage.

In ECG terms, a 'lead' refers to the difference in voltage recorded between pairs of electrodes placed on the patient's skin. The number of leads used to produce an ECG varies, with 3-, 5- and 12-lead ECGs being the most common; 3- and 5-lead ECGs are generally used for continuous monitoring of a patient, with the output displayed on a screen. A 12-lead ECG is traditionally printed out on paper as a one-off picture of the heart.

Ten electrodes are used to produce a 12-lead ECG recording. One electrode is placed on each of the four limbs. The remaining six electrodes are placed on the chest wall, starting just to the right of the sternum and moving left across the chest. A 12-lead ECG allows a visualisation of the heart from different angles.

An electroencephalogram (EEG) operates on the same principles as an ECG but with the electrodes placed on the scalp. An EEG is a recording, taken over a time period of between 20 and 40 minutes, of the electrical activity of the brain. Diagnostically, EEGs are most often used in epilepsy. They can also be used to detect brain activity in comatose patients and in sleep studies. They are no longer used in the diagnosis of brain tumours or stroke as MRI or CT scans provide better, more precise images.

Investigative Procedures – Systems

Cardiovascular system

Plain chest X-ray

With respect to the cardiovascular system, a plain chest X-ray (CXR) is done to observe the size and position of the heart and the large blood vessels. For a plain CXR to be of use in assessing these factors, the film should be taken with the patient sitting or standing erect. An isolated plain CXR may not be of great value, whereas a series of films will highlight any changes in cardiac size.

Echocardiogram

Ultrasonic examination of the heart produces a two-dimensional view of the chambers and valves in motion. This allows the thickness and contractility of the walls of the heart and the size of each of the chambers to be studied. Cardiac valve patency can also be assessed.

ECG

As discussed on page 28, an ECG is used to monitor the electrical activity of the heart and highlight any abnormalities in beat and rhythm. It may also be performed over 24 hours to detect any unusual events – an ambulatory ECG, sometimes known as a '24-hour tape'.

Radionuclide imaging

Myocardial perfusion scintigraphy involves the intravenous injection of a radiopharmaceutical which is taken up by the myocardium in proportion to the blood flow to the tissue. This allows areas of reduced myocardial perfusion, usually the result of ischaemic damage, to be seen. This technique is used in patients who have suspected or known ischaemic chest pain. As myocardial perfusion is increased during exercise, the first image is taken during an exercise test with the images repeated after a rest period of three to four hours. The contrast in perfusion between the two images will identify areas of ischaemic or infarcted tissue.

PET scans, utilising FDG, provide information on glucose metabolism in the myocardium. As with perfusion scintigraphy, areas of viable and non-viable myocardial tissue will be imaged.

MRI

MRI scans are particularly useful for identifying congenital (present from birth) heart defects as they give very detailed images of heart wall movement.

Cardiac catheterisation

Cardiac catheterisation is a powerful diagnostic tool involving the insertion of a long, hollow, radiopaque catheter in an artery or vein which is manipulated up to and within the heart and great vessels under X-ray control. It is used to investigate coronary heart disease, valvular heart disease and congenital heart disease.

CT

This is a very complex procedure and is more technically demanding due to the need to study cardiac motion and function as well as structure.

Respiratory system

Plain CXR

A plain CXR for examination of the respiratory system comprises a frontal (posteroanterior) view and a side (lateral) view. Both are taken on full inspiration with the patient sitting upright or standing. Full inspiration is important as this provides a clear image of the lung bases and prevents the size of the heart appearing enlarged.

In a normal CXR, the size and position of the heart should be normal. The only structures within the lungs that should be visible are the blood vessels, interlobal fissures and the walls of some of the larger bronchi. The bones of the chest should be intact (the ribs, sternum, clavicles and spine). It is difficult to isolate small lesions (less than 1 cm in size) on a plain CXR as they are often hidden by other structures in the chest.

Acute bacterial pneumonia will be evident as opacities on a plain CXR. An opacity is an air space that is filled with fluid, blood or pus. Opacities have poorly defined edges. In bacterial pneumonia there is usually consolidation of all, or the majority, of a lobe of a lung. An air bronchogram may also be visible. Normally air in bronchi is not visible on a plain CXR but if a bronchiole is surrounded by fluid-filled alveoli, a contrast will be seen between the air in the bronchiole and the surrounding fluid.

A plain CXR will also show reductions in lung volume through bronchial obstruction, pneumothorax or pleural effusion.

Single nodules seen within the lungs may be indicative of bronchial carcinoma, benign tumours, infective granuloma (most commonly due to tuberculosis), lung abscess or metastasis. Further tests such as PET scans, CT or biopsy are necessary to arrive at a diagnosis.

A 'speckled' appearance of the lungs is due to multiple small opacities (less than 2 mm in size). The possible causes of such speckling include miliary tuberculosis, sarcoidosis, asbestosis and interstitial pulmonary fibrosis.

Bronchoscopy

Bronchoscopy is the inspection of the interior of the tracheobronchial tree using either a flexible or a rigid bronchoscope inserted through the nose or mouth. The technique allows the visualisation of abnormalities such as bleeding, tumours, inflammation or foreign bodies. Tissue biopsies may also be taken using bronchoscopy.

CT

CT will show up consolidation, air bronchograms, abscesses, lung collapse, tumours, pleural fluid and pneumothorax. Computed tomography pulmonary angiography, where an intravenous contrast agent is used, is an imaging technique used to identify pulmonary emboli in large and medium-sized pulmonary vessels.

Radionuclide scans

Radionuclide imaging is no longer routinely used for the diagnosis of pulmonary embolism as CT scanning provides better, higher-resolution images. Ventilation/perfusion scanning is used to identify causes of perfusion defects such as pulmonary oedema, pneumonia, tumours or emphysema. A perfusion scan observes the distribution of ^{99m}Tc within the lungs following intravenous injection. A ventilation scan observes the distribution of inhaled ^{81m}Kr within the lungs. If any observed deficiencies match on both scans, the diagnosis is most likely to be pneumonia, pulmonary oedema or airway disease such as emphysema. Mismatched scans are likely to be due to pulmonary emboli. However in practice radionuclide lung scans are often inconclusive.

Respiratory function testing

Measurement of lung function is a useful tool in the diagnosis and monitoring of lung disease. A series of tests can be performed to assess lung function. These routine tests are performed using a spirometer, hence the more common name of spirometry.

The tests include:

Forced expiratory volume (FEV). The patient is asked to breathe in as deeply as possible and then blow out as forcefully as possible through the spirometer. *FEV1* is the volume of air exhaled in the first second of this forced exhalation. The *forced vital capacity (FVC)* is the volume of air blown out with maximum effort after maximum inspiration. The ratio of FEV1 to FVC provides a very useful and easily reproducible indicator of lung performance in any individual. Patients with normal lung function are usually capable of exhaling approximately 75% of their FVC in the first second. This figure is then used as a benchmark for deterioration or improvement in lung function. It is also an indicator of airway obstruction (for example in an asthma attack).

A peak flow meter is used by patients for self-assessment purposes. This is not as accurate as a spirometer but is a very useful tool nonetheless. Peak flow meters measure the *peak expiratory flow rate (PEFR)* upon forced exhalation rather than a volume. As with FEV1 and FVC, the PEFR can be used to monitor disease control or progression. All three measures vary with age, gender, height and weight, and tables exist for comparison purposes.

Gastrointestinal system

Plain abdominal X-ray

Plain abdominal films are taken as a frontal view with the patient supine. They are very useful in the diagnosis of intestinal obstruction, as intestinal gas collects behind the obstruction, dilating loops of bowel. In a normal bowel there will be small patches of gas evident but rarely sufficient to dilate a whole loop. Perforation of the bowel will be evident on a plain film as free gas in the peritoneum.

Plain films are not of any great use in the diagnosis of abdominal masses. The liver and spleen have to be greatly enlarged to be apparent.

Contrast examinations, usually using barium sulphate as the contrast medium, are used to highlight the mucosal surfaces of the bowel. For the stomach and the small bowel, the barium sulphate is ingested orally. For studies of the large bowel, it is administered rectally. However barium studies have largely been superseded by endoscopy.

CT

CT scans, often using contrast agents (including air, gas and Gastrografin), are used to diagnose and stage GI tumours. They are also used to monitor complications of surgery or chemotherapy and in the diagnosis of appendicitis, traumatic damage to the bowel and intestinal obstruction.

Ultrasound

Ultrasound is of limited use for examining the patency of the bowel but it is used in the diagnosis of infantile pyloric stenosis and intussusception. Suspected appendicitis with few clinical symptoms may be diagnosed with ultrasound.

MRI

Generally MRI is only used for the assessment of the local spread of rectal carcinoma and of anal fistulae and abscesses. Otherwise the peristaltic movement of the gut causes imaging problems in MRI.

Endoscopy

Endoscopy is the gold standard technique for the investigation of: acute upper GI haemorrhage, oesophageal strictures, peptic ulcer disease, dysphagia, gastric ulcers, Crohn's disease, ulcerative colitis and colorectal tumours.

Liver, spleen and biliary tract

Plain abdominal X-ray

Plain X-ray films are not of great use in diagnostic imaging of the liver, spleen and biliary tract. The liver and spleen have to be greatly enlarged to be visible and approximately 80% of gall stones are cholesterol-based and so are radiolucent.

Ultrasound

An abdominal ultrasound scan (USS) is often the initial scanning technique used. Cysts and solid masses in the liver are both visible on USS. Cirrhosis of the liver is usually seen as a reduction in size of the right lobe and an abnormal texture of the surface of the liver. Ascites, if present, will also be apparent. Traumatic liver damage results in free fluid in the perihepatic and perisplenic spaces, the pelvis and the pericardium. USS is the imaging technique for the identification of this free fluid.

USS can identify gall stones greater than 1 mm in size and will also show the common bile duct allowing abnormalities to be identified.

Examining the spleen is less useful as the spleen has a very similar echo density to the liver.

CT

CT scans of the liver are usually performed with contrast media to differentiate normal liver tissue from abnormalities such as abscesses or tumours. All of the structures of the biliary system can be seen on a CT scan but abdominal ultrasound produces better information and so is preferred.

CT is ideal for imaging the pancreas as the structure is often obscured by other abdominal organs in other imaging techniques. It is also an excellent method for imaging the spleen, particularly if it is suspected there is traumatic damage.

MRI

As with CT, MRI is useful for detecting abnormalities within the liver, including cysts, abscesses and tumours. A form of MRI – magnetic resonance cholangiopancreatography (MRCP) – is used to visualise the pancreatic and biliary ducts. It is non-invasive and does not involve the use of contrast media. If a biopsy is required, endoscopic retrograde cholangiopancreatography (ERCP) is the preferred method. In ERCP a duodenoscope is inserted into the junction of the pancreatic and bile ducts and contrast medium is used to outline the ducts.

Nervous system – skull and brain

Plain skull X-ray

Apart from skeletal survey following head and/or neck trauma, plain X-ray films of the skull are rarely taken as they provide little relevant diagnostic information.

CT

A CT scan of the head usually consists of between 20 and 30 sections, 3 to 5 millimetres thick. These sections are taken in the axial plane (horizontally through the skull). Contrast media can be used to enhance brain lesions where the blood brain barrier (BBB) is no longer intact; the BBB usually prevents the passage of contrast media into brain tissue. Such lesions include areas of inflammation, ischaemia and neoplasms.

MRI

MRI scans produce extremely detailed images of all structures within the skull. They are particularly useful for imaging the pituitary gland and other structures in the base of the skull which are difficult to pick up on CT scans. A major disadvantage of MRI is that equipment used on patients who are intubated and monitored must be MRI compatible.

Nervous system – spine

Plain X-ray

A plain X-ray film of the spine can identify some spinal pathologies such as fractures, vertebral collapse, disc space narrowing and sclerosis. However other imaging techniques are usually required to confirm a diagnosis.

CT

CT scans are useful for identifying fine fractures within the vertebrae that are difficult to pick up on plain X-ray films.

MRI

MRI is the gold standard method for imaging the spine. This is because structures such as the spinal cord, intervertebral discs and nerve roots can all be visualised clearly. These structures are poorly seen on CT scans and are not visible on plain films.

Urinary system

Ultrasound

Ultrasound is the main imaging technique for the renal system as it can visualise the anatomy without the need for ionising radiation. USS can give a clear picture of the size and position of the kidneys, renal tumours, renal abscesses and cysts, renal scarring, renal length, the bladder and the prostate gland. Bladder scans are usually performed with a full bladder to provide a sharp outline of the bladder walls.

CT

CT scans using intravenous iodinated contrast media (CT urography) are performed to investigate renal calculi (stones), causes of haematuria, renal masses, suspected renal trauma and to stage and follow up renal carcinoma.

MRI

MRI is usually only used in specific renal or urinary conditions as calcification (a common cause of renal problems) is not visible on MRI. It can be used to assess bladder and prostate cancers prior to surgery, renal artery stenosis or the extent of renal tumours.

Radionuclide scanning

Radionuclide scanning (a renogram) is used to measure renal function: ^{99m}Tc radiopharmaceuticals which are filtered by the glomeruli and/or secreted by the renal tubules are injected intravenously. The patient is scanned by a gamma camera positioned posteriorly. Early images show the major blood vessels and as time passes the kidneys become visible, followed by the collecting systems and finally the bladder. A curve of renal activity over time can be plotted and the kidneys compared to one another.

Section 4
Laboratory reports

Reports from medical laboratories have a two-fold function. They are used to give an indication of disease state and also to monitor patient progress. If report forms are printed, they are often colour coded and are found in a separate section of the patient's medical notes. However these reports are often held electronically rather than as a hard copy.

Reference Ranges

Each laboratory has its own set of reference values based on the population of the area that it serves. The reference ranges included in this book are for guidance only as there will be local variations.

A result outside the reference range may be caused not only by the disease state (if present) but also by drug therapy, the time the sample was taken, sample technique, recent exercise, age, gender and diet.

Therefore, a single result outside the normal reference range should be compared with other results for the patient to identify a trend. The test may be repeated if the result is wildly different from others for that patient or if there are no other results available.

Medical Laboratories

The laboratories included in this section are those that are of the most relevance to the clinical pharmacist, namely: clinical chemistry (biochemistry), haematology and microbiology. Summaries of the reference values for each laboratory are provided in Tables 4.1 and 4.2. Note that all reference values quoted are for adults; for paediatric values other sources should be consulted.

Table 4.1: Clinical chemistry reference ranges

Parameter	Reference range
Sodium	135–145 mmol/L
Potassium	3.5–5.0 mmol/L

Calcium (ionised)	1.0–1.25 mmol/L
Calcium (total)	2.12–2.65 mmol/L (must be corrected for albumin)
Magnesium	0.75–1.05 mmol/L
Bicarbonate	24–30 mmol/L
Chloride	95–105 mmol/L
Urea	2.5–7.5 mmol/L
Creatinine	50–130 micromoles/L
Creatinine clearance	90–125 mL/min
Blood glucose (fingerprick)	4–8 mmol/L
HbA1c	< 48 mmol/mol
Bilirubin	5–17 micromoles/L
Alkaline phosphatase (Alk. Phos.)	40–160 IU/L
AST	< 45 IU/L
ALT	< 40 IU/L
Gamma GT	< 40 IU/L
Albumin	35–47 g/L
Total cholesterol (TC)	< 5 mmol/L fasting
LDL cholesterol	< 3 mmol/L fasting
HDL cholesterol	> 1.2 mmol/L
TC : HDL ratio	≤ 4.5
Triglycerides	< 1.7 mmol/L fasting
TSH	0.4–4.5 milliunits/L (mU/L)
Free T4	9.0–25.0 picomoles/L (pmol/L)
Free T3	3.5–7.8 picomoles/L (pmol/L)
Troponin T	Myocardial damage: 0.03–0.1 mcg/L Myocardial infarction: ≥ 0.1 mcg/L
Troponin I	Myocardial damage: 0.15–1.5 mcg/L Myocardial infarction: ≥1.5 mcg/L
CKMB	< 25 IU/L

Table 4.2: Haematology reference ranges

Parameter	Reference range
RBC	Male: 4.5–6.5 x 10^{12}/L Female: 3.8–5.8 x 10^{12}/L
PCV	Male: 40–52% Female: 37–47%
MCV	76–96 femtolitres (fl)
Haemoglobin	Male: 135–180 g/L Female: 114–165 g/L
MCH	27–32 picograms (pg)
MCHC	33–37 g/dL
WBC	4–11 x 10^9/L
Neutrophils	2–7.5 x 10^9/L
Platelets	150–400 x 10^9/L
ESR	< 10 mm/hr (rises with age)
CRP	< 10 mg/L
Prothrombin time	12–16 seconds
aPPT	35–45 seconds (variable according to laboratory)
D-dimers	0.3–0.5 mg/L

Clinical Chemistry

Urea and electrolytes (U&Es)

The U&Es consist of the routine blood chemistry profile. Sodium, potassium and urea can provide an indication of the fluid balance of a patient. Low sodium, potassium and urea concentrations indicate an excess of water (fluid overload). High concentrations of the above may indicate a deficit of water (dehydration).

Artificially high levels of potassium may occur when haemolysis of the blood sample occurs due to incorrect technique when taking the blood sample. Blood cells are damaged and release the intracellular potassium. If a sample is haemolysed, it is recorded on the report form.

Indicators of renal function

Urea is the end product of metabolism. High levels may occur as a result of decreased excretion due to renal impairment. However, high values may also occur due to catabolism (increased protein breakdown), e.g. in pyrexia, post-operatively, patients on high-protein diets, dehydration, gastrointestinal bleeding and decreased liver function.

Creatinine is an end product of muscle metabolism and is produced at a constant rate. It is eliminated almost completely by the kidney and can therefore give a very good indication of renal function, with high levels generally indicating renal impairment. However, very low levels may occur in the elderly, the frail and those with muscle wasting. Therefore, the creatinine clearance is of more value.

Glomerular filtration rate (GFR) is an indication of renal function but the estimations of GFR are only valid when serum creatinine levels are stable. GFR is measured using the rate the kidneys excrete creatinine (creatinine clearance – CrCl). Low creatinine clearance values tend to indicate renal impairment. Creatinine clearance can be measured practically or estimated mathematically.

In the practical measurement of creatinine clearance, all urine passed by the patient is collected for 24 hours. A blood sample requesting the creatinine level is taken at the start of the 24-hour period. From this the laboratory obtains a value for the level of creatinine in the blood at time zero, the concentration of creatinine excreted into the urine over 24 hours and the volume of urine passed in 24 hours. These three pieces of data allow the calculation of creatinine clearance for a patient.

Mathematical estimates of creatinine clearance can be calculated using several methods. Creatinine clearance is most commonly reported by laboratories in the UK as an estimated GFR (eGFR) based upon the MDRD equation and this is the measure used in the British National Formulary. It is a very complex calculation and is performed by the laboratory and reported back directly; eGFR is only valid in certain groups of patients.

CrCl can also be estimated by using the Cockcroft and Gault equation. This is only valid in patients aged 18 years or over. There is an equation for female and male patients.

Women:

$$\text{Creatinine clearance (mL/min)} = \frac{1.04 \times (140 - \text{age}) \times \text{body weight (kg)}}{\text{Plasma creatinine (mol/L)}}$$

Men:

$$\text{Creatinine clearance (mL/min)} = \frac{1.23 \times (140 - \text{age}) \times \text{body weight (kg)}}{\text{Plasma creatinine (mol/L)}}$$

These equations can only be used as a guide and are only validated for use in certain individuals. For patients with renal impairment, drug dose adjustments may need to be made – nephrotoxic agents, chemotherapy and drugs with a narrow therapeutic index – and the Cockcroft and Gault equation may need to be used to calculate these. Each case should be given individual consideration based on the patient's parameters and the medication concerned.

Blood glucose can be measured using the fingerprick test. In the UK, the fingerprick test is often referred to by healthcare professionals as 'BMs', as some of the first test strips developed to monitor blood glucose levels were manufactured by Boehringer-Mannheim (BM-Test strips).

In non-diabetic patients, blood glucose levels are maintained between 4 and 8 mmol/L. In diabetic patients, blood glucose levels may be more erratic but pre-prandial levels of between 4 and 7 mmol/L are aimed for. The typical blood glucose target levels are shown in Table 4.3.

Table 4.3: Typical blood glucose targets for adult patients

Sampling time for blood glucose	Blood glucose reading (mmol/L)		
	Non-diabetic	*Type I diabetes*	*Type 2 diabetes*
Before meals	3.5–5.0	4.0–7.0	4.0–7.0
Two hours after meals	< 8.0	< 8.5	< 9.0

Glycosylated haemoglobin (HbA$_{1c}$) is produced when haemoglobin is exposed to plasma glucose. If the amount of plasma glucose is elevated this will produce a higher proportion of glycosylated haemoglobin. The HbA$_{1c}$ test is therefore a useful way of monitoring the diabetic control of patients over a period of 2 to 3 months. A higher HbA$_{1c}$ value indicates poor control of plasma glucose in the preceding 2 to 3 months.

Indicators of liver function (Liver Function Tests, LFTs)

LFTs are useful in determining whether the liver is diseased and whether the hepatic cells or the biliary system are involved. LFTs indicate the extent and progress of liver disease, not the actual liver function. Liver function is better estimated by examination of albumin levels and clotting.

Bilirubin is the main bile pigment resulting from the catabolism of haem-containing proteins. Increased bilirubin causes jaundice (yellow pigmentation of eyes and skin) by being deposited just below the skin surface. The increase may be due to increased production (e.g. haemolysis) or defective elimination (blocked bile duct, impaired liver function). It is therefore necessary to consider bilirubin results along with other LFTs to determine the problem.

Bilirubin levels are an accurate measure of the depth of jaundice. Sustained high levels may be associated with malignant disease, whilst fluctuating high levels are more commonly due to gall stones.

Liver enzymes. Liver cells contain many enzymes that may be released into the blood stream when cell damage occurs. None are specific to the liver and so must be considered along with other results and interpreted carefully.

Alkaline phosphatase (Alk. phos) occurs in almost all tissues, particularly bone and the intestine. Small increases may indicate cell damage (relatively little alk. phos is released when liver cell damage occurs). Large increases may indicate obstruction of the biliary tract or bone conditions such as Paget's disease, bone metastases, bone fractures or osteosarcoma.

The aminotransferase results reported by clinical chemistry are *aspartate aminotransferase* (AST) and alanine aminotransferase (ALT). These are present mainly in the cytoplasm of hepatocytes and can therefore give an indication of cell integrity (damaged or killed). The highest levels are found in acute liver disease (e.g. viral hepatitis) where levels are up to 100 times normal values. In obstructive jaundice, levels rarely rise above five times normal values.

Gamma glutamyl transferase (GT, Gamma GT) is a microsomal enzyme in body tissues and it is a sensitive index. The highest levels occur in biliary obstruction, but there is also a marked increase in acute parenchymal damage. Microsomal inducing agents such as phenytoin and alcohol may also increase the level. Therefore it can be used to detect and follow alcohol abuse with little other liver function abnormality.

Albumin is a plasma protein synthesised solely in the liver. It has a long half-life (20-26 days) and so changes in concentration are slow. Low levels may be found in chronic liver disease such as cirrhosis and are generally found in patients with more severe liver damage, and decreasing levels are a sign of a poor prognosis.

There are unlikely to be any changes in levels in acute liver disease. Albumin levels can also be affected by other factors such as malnutrition and renal disease.

Lipid profile

A lipid profile can be used to determine a patient's risk of developing heart disease. The lipid profile includes a range of tests: total cholesterol, LDL cholesterol, HDL cholesterol and triglycerides.

Total cholesterol is the total amount of cholesterol in a blood sample. Cholesterol is a fatty substance that is produced by the liver and is vital for the body to function normally. However having high levels in the blood can lead to accumulation in the artery walls and over time narrowing of the arteries.

Cholesterol is carried in the blood, bound to lipoproteins: low density lipoproteins (LDL) and high density lipoproteins (HDL). LDL cholesterol is often referred to as 'bad' cholesterol and HDL cholesterol as 'good' cholesterol. *LDL cholesterol* carries cholesterol from the liver to the cells that need it. If there is too much cholesterol for the cells to use, this can build up in the artery walls. *HDL cholesterol* carries cholesterol away from cells to the liver, where it can be broken down and excreted from the body.

The TC:HDL ratio is the total serum cholesterol level divided by the serum HDL cholesterol level. A low ratio value indicates that the patient has more HDL than LDL cholesterol in their blood, which is desirable.

Triglycerides are the end product of the breakdown and digestion of dietary fats. They are the main form in which fat is stored in the body.

Thyroid function tests

Thyroid function tests (TFTs) are a range of tests which allow the function of the thyroid gland to be checked. These include thyroid stimulating hormone (TSH), free T4 (FT4) and free T3 (FT3).

Thyroid stimulating hormone (TSH) is released from the pituitary gland in response to low levels of thyroid hormones in the blood. The release of TSH activates the thyroid to produce more thyroid hormones. *Free T_4* (thyroxine) is released from the thyroid gland and is then converted to tri-iodothyronine (*free T_3*), the biologically active form of thyroid hormone which contributes to metabolic regulation.

Indicators of myocardial infarction

Death of heart tissue (for example, following a myocardial infarction) produces a detectable rise in proteins that are normally confined to cardiac cells. The cell death also produces rises in several enzymes which are not necessarily cardiospecific but can give a good indication of cell damage.

Cardiac troponins (cTnI or cTnT). Which of the two cardiac troponins are reported depends very much upon the equipment used by the reporting laboratory. The immunoassay for troponin I is currently under patent to Roche and so can only be performed on Roche equipment. There are several immunoassays available for troponin T, which can be used on a variety of equipment, and so troponin T is the most commonly reported of the two. High sensitivity troponin (hs-cTn) tests are now available, making it possible to identify those patients presenting with acute coronary syndromes earlier. Troponin is the preferred indicator of myocardial damage. Levels are usually measured on admission and a second measurement is taken 6–9 hours after admission. Further samples may be required after 12–24 hours. If a 20% increase in troponin levels is seen on the second measurement, then cardiac damage is confirmed. Troponin levels peak within 24 hours of an MI and fall gradually over 10 days. Levels of greater than 50 times normal are supportive of an MI, whilst lower raised levels are indicative of myocardial damage, possibly from another cause. Cardiac troponin levels are summarised in Table 4.4.

Table 4.4: Cardiac troponin levels

	Troponin T	**Troponin I**
Normal	< 0.03 mcg/L	< 0.15 mcg/L
Myocardial damage	0.03–0.1 mcg/L	0.15–1.5 mcg/L
Supportive of myocardial infarction	≥ 0.1 mcg/L	≥ 1.5 mcg/L

The troponin tests utilised by each Trust may differ and so in clinical practice the local Trust policy for reporting ranges and sampling times post-admission should be consulted.

Creatinine kinase (CK) is also present in skeletal muscle as well as cardiac muscle and so increases can also be due to intra-muscular (IM) injection or vigorous exercise. Therefore, the usual measurement is the cardiac specific *creatinine kinase myocardial isoenzyme* (CKMB). The level of CKMB begins to rise 4 to 6 hours post-MI, peaking 12 hours post-MI and returning to normal 48 to 72 hours post-MI.

Aspartate aminotransferase levels begin to rise 12 hours post-MI, peaking during the first or second day post-MI.

Lactate dehydrogenase (LDH) is a less specific indicator of myocardial damage as it is also released from haemolysed blood cells. However it can be useful when the diagnosis of MI is uncertain several days after an episode of chest pain. LDH levels begin to rise 12 hours post-MI, peaking two to three days post-MI and returning to normal about one week post-MI.

B-type natriuretic peptide (BNP) is a neurohormone secreted mainly by the cardiac ventricles in response to cardiac stress and overload. It is a useful measurement in symptomatic patients suspected of having heart failure. Levels are interpreted thus:

- < 100 pg/mL (< 29 pmol/mL) = normal
- 100–400 pg/mL (29–116 pmol/mL) – refer the patient for an echocardiogram
- > 400 pg/mL (> 116 pmol/mL) – urgent referral for echocardiogram as the levels denote a poor prognosis

Haematology

Erythrocytes

Reports concerning the red blood cells (RBC) are usually of interest in anaemia. This is the state in which the level of haemoglobin (Hb) in the blood is lower than expected, taking into account the age and sex of the patient.

The type of anaemia can be determined by investigating the number, size and shape, and haemoglobin content of red blood cells.

The red blood cell count is performed electronically. A *decreased* count is indicative of megaloblastic anaemias (e.g. vitamin B12 deficiency) or folate deficiency, or both.

A *normal* or only slightly decreased count with symptoms of anaemia is indicative of iron deficiency anaemia.

The *packed cell volume* (PCV or *haematocrit*) is calculated by centrifuging a tube of blood under standard conditions. The height of the column of red blood cells at the bottom of the tube, as a proportion of the total height of the column, is the PCV. The PCV is affected by a variation of plasma volume: either expansion (cardiac failure, pregnancy) or contraction (due to diuretics).

The size and shape of red blood cells is determined by microscopy of a blood film. This can also give an indication of haemoglobin content. Smaller (*microcytic*) cells are indicative of iron deficiency anaemia or thalassaemia. Larger (*macrocytic*) cells are suggestive of megaloblastic anaemias. Irregular (*poikilocytic*) cells are usually the result of severe iron deficiency or pernicious anaemia.

The *mean cell volume* (MCV) is an indicator of RBC size and is obtained electronically. A decreased MCV (small cells) suggests iron deficiency anaemia, whilst an increased MCV (large cells) is indicative of megaloblastic anaemia.

Decreased *haemoglobin* (Hb) values (hypochromic cells) may indicate the presence of anaemia. The symptoms of anaemia depend on severity, but also on how rapidly the anaemia appears. Patients who have symptoms of anaemia but normal Hb values (normochromic cells) are more likely to have a megaloblastic anaemia.

The *mean cell haemoglobin* (MCH) is an indicator of the amount of Hb in the cell and is derived from the Hb and red blood cell count. A decreased MCH is suggestive of iron deficiency anaemia and an increased MCH megaloblastic anaemia.

The *mean cell haemoglobin concentration* (MCHC) is the concentration of Hb in the red blood cell. It is based on the PCV, which is more accurate than the RBC count. A decreased MCHC suggests iron deficiency anaemia, whilst a normal MCHC is an indicator of a megaloblastic anaemia (there is a reduced number of red blood cells, but the cells are larger, with a normal concentration of Hb).

A summary of the diagnostic uses of red blood cell counts in patients with symptoms of anaemia is provided in Table 4.5.

Table 4.5: Diagnostic uses of red blood cell counts

Red blood cell characteristics	Likely diagnosis
Microcytic, hypochromic	Iron deficiency anaemia
Macrocytic, normochromic	Megaloblastic anaemia
Normocytic, normochromic	Malignancy, infection, leukaemia

Anaemia is a chronic lowering of haemoglobin levels. It should also be remembered that decreased haemoglobin levels will be recorded in patients who have had severe blood loss through trauma or surgery; long-term replacement therapy is not required in such patients.

Leucocytes

Since the main function of leucocytes is defence, striking changes in the total white blood cell (WBC) count are seen in infections and inflammation. It should be remembered that the WBC is very variable in normal individuals – counts are decreased in the morning and at rest, and may be increased by stress and affected by changes in the menstrual cycle.

A decreased WBC (leucopenia) is often caused by bone marrow failure, including suppression due to drugs or a marked enlargement of the spleen. An increased WBC is seen in most bacterial infections, (counts may be as high as 50×10^9/L in acute infections) and after injury. Much higher counts may be found in leukaemia, particularly chronic leukaemia, but counts are variable in acute leukaemia.

A differential white cell count is often reported along with the WBC. It is obtained by the analysis of the different types of leucocytes in a total of 200 to 300 cells. There are three types of white blood cells: polymorphonuclear leucocytes (neutrophils, eosinophils and basophils), lymphocytes and monocytes.

Neutrophils are the most abundant form of white blood cell, accounting for between 40% and 75% of the WBC. A decreased number of neutrophils (neutropenia, or agranulocytosis in its most severe form) usually follows excessive irradiation and/or the use of cytotoxic drugs. An increased neutrophil count occurs in bacterial infections, inflammatory conditions and tissue damage.

Eosinophils make up between 1% and 6% of the total WBC. An increase in eosinophils (eosinophilia) occurs in allergic conditions such as asthma, hay fever and drug allergies, and may also occur in parasitic infections, malignant disease and irradiation.

Basophils make up less than 1% of the total WBC. An increase in basophils (basophilia) occurs in viral infections, chronic myeloid leukaemia, malignancy and myxoedema.

Lymphocytes are the second most common form of WBC, accounting for between 20% and 45% of the total WBC. Lymphocyte levels are generally only raised in certain viral infections such as mumps, infectious hepatitis and infectious mononucleosis (glandular fever).

Monocytes (2% to 10% of the WBC) are macrophages and so are increased in acute and chronic infections, malignancy and chronic inflammation.

Platelets

Platelets are small fragments of precursor cells produced by the bone marrow. As such their levels are indicative of bone marrow function. Decreased platelet numbers (thrombocytopenia) are usually due to defective platelet production caused by bone marrow suppression, although slight decreases may be seen in pregnancy or viral infections. Levels below $100 \times 10^9/L$ are clinically significant and levels below $40 \times 10^9/l$ commonly result in spontaneous bleeding into the skin and mucous membranes producing purpura. Increased platelet numbers (thrombocytosis) may occur transiently after injury and surgery.

Other values

Erythrocyte sedimentation rate

When blood is treated with an anticoagulant and left to stand, the red blood cells will slowly sediment out. The rate at which they do so is the known as the *erythrocyte sedimentation rate* (ESR). If certain proteins cover the red blood cells, they will stick to each other in columns and fall faster, thus increasing the ESR.

An increased ESR may be a non-specific indicator of disease. In patients with a slightly raised ESR, the plan is usually to wait a month and repeat the test as it is affected by many other factors including age, anaemia, drugs. A markedly increased ESR (> 100 mm/hr) is usually caused by connective tissue diseases, rheumatoid arthritis, renal disease, infection or disseminated malignancy. A decrease in the ESR is usually due to heart failure, polycythaemia or sickle cell anaemia.

C-reactive protein

C-reactive protein (CRP) is produced by the liver in response to inflammatory cytokines. A rise in CRP levels is a general marker for infection and inflammation and the CRP can be used as a series of measurements to monitor disease progress in response to treatment. CRP levels in the blood rise more quickly than the ESR and therefore the CRP measurement is more commonly used to detect inflammation due to acute causes (e.g. infection) and exacerbations of chronic inflammatory conditions.

Prothrombin time

Prothrombin time is an indicator of the extrinsic clotting pathway (measuring factors I, II, V, VII and X). A blood sample is centrifuged to obtain plasma and Tissue factor (factor III) is added. The time taken for the plasma to clot is measured in seconds. This result varies for individuals according to the method of analysis used by the testing laboratory.

International Normalised Ratio

The *international normalised ratio* (INR) was developed to standardise the results of prothrombin time testing. It is a measure of the time it takes blood to clot against a control. An international sensitivity index (ISI) is applied to the result to standardise the different commercial testing systems used. Treatment with anticoagulants prolongs the time taken for blood to clot and so increases the INR. Different conditions require different INR values for successful treatment.

A typically 'normal' reported INR range in a non-anticoagulated adult patient is 0.9–1.1. Guidance on target INRs is given in the British Committee for Standards in Haematology (BCSH) guidelines. For example, patients who present with a deep vein thrombosis (DVT) will have a target INR of 2.5 (range = 2.0–3.0)

D-dimers

D-dimer is a fibrin degradation product (FDP) which is generated as a result of a blood clot being broken down by the body. Elevated D-dimer levels usually indicate the presence of a blood clot such as in deep vein thrombosis (DVT) or pulmonary embolism (PE). The presentation of the results of a D-dimer test depends upon the type of analytical equipment used by the laboratory. Typically a reading of < 350 ng/mL is interpreted as a negative result (i.e. no clot present), whilst readings of ≥ 350 ng/mL are interpreted as a positive result (i.e. a clot is present). The size of the 'positive' value is not necessarily indicative of the size of the blood clot; the clinical symptoms presented by the patient should also be taken into account. A suspected DVT should be confirmed with a Doppler ultrasound scan, whilst a suspected PE should be confirmed either by computed tomography pulmonary angiography (CTPA) or a lung ventilation perfusion (VQ) scan of the lungs.

Activated partial thromboplastin time

The *activated partial thromboplastin time* (aPPT) is a measure of the intrinsic clotting pathway and is used to monitor patients being treated with unfractionated heparin. Patients receiving low molecular weight heparins (LMWHs) do not require aPPT monitoring.

Anti-factor Xa

Anti-factor Xa testing measures anti-activated X (ant-Xa) and can be used to monitor and adjust the doses, if necessary, of low molecular weight heparins (LMWH). LMWH anticoagulation is not routinely monitored but in certain patient groups, such as pregnant women and patients with kidney disease, monitoring may be desirable. The target range for ant-Xa is typically 0.5–0.8 IU/mL.

Urinalysis

Urine testing is a simple, non-invasive, reliable method of detecting abnormalities and may lead the health practitioner to detect potential disease at an early stage. Urine abnormalities can be detected using reagent test strips and may show either abnormally high levels of a substance in the blood, exceeding the capacity for normal tubular reabsorption (e.g. glucose, ketones), or altered kidney function (e.g. proteinuria).

Urinalysis has three functions: screening (e.g. random glucose testing for diabetes), diagnosis (e.g. primary and secondary renal disease), monitoring (e.g. disease progression, drug toxicity, drug compliance and illicit drug use).

Table 4.6 summarises the substances that can be screened using general urine analysis.

Table 4.6: Substances screened in general urine analysis

Substance	Suggestive of:
Protein	Hypertension, pre-eclampsia, glomerulonephritis, infection
Blood (not normally present)	Infection, renal calculi, injury, malignancy
Ketones (breakdown of fatty acids)	Anorexia, uncontrolled diabetes
Nitrite (best in early morning sample)	Infection
Glucose	Raised blood glucose levels or abnormal excretion
Urobilinogen	Liver disease
Bilirubin	Biliary disease

Collection of urine

The most frequent type of urine sample is a 'mid-stream urine' sample (MSU). The patient should be asked to clean themselves, pass urine into the toilet, before collecting 10–20 ml in the container (i.e. mid-stream), and then continue voiding into the toilet. Urine may also be collected for analysis from patients who are catheterised. This is called a catheter specimen (CSU). The urine should be collected from the drainage bag, using a syringe and needle, from the specimen port on the drainage bag. The port should be wiped with an alcohol wipe before the sample is collected.

Performing urinalysis

Observation

The urine specimen should be less than 4 hours old. If necessary it may be stored in a fridge but not a freezer. Before testing, the sample is examined for smell, colour, clarity and other abnormalities. Urine may vary in colour but a normal sample is usually straw-coloured and clear. Any cloudiness may represent abnormalities such as the presence of pus (pyuria). Alternatively urine that has been left to stand may start to precipitate out phosphate and urate salts. Fresh urine has little smell but after a few hours it may smell like ammonia. If an infection is present the urine may smell 'fishy'. Other factors can influence both the appearance and smell of urine. Some drugs, such as sulfasalazine and rifampicin may change the colour of urine, and asparagus can impart a characteristic smell.

Testing with reagent strips

Reagent strips may test for single factors, most commonly glucose and ketones, or they may be multifunctional.

Table 4.7 summarises common medical terminology used in relation to urine.

Table 4.7: Common medical terminology in relation to urine

Term	Meaning
Anuria	No urine output
Dysuria	Pain or discomfort in passing urine
Glycosuria	Glucose in urine
Haematuria	Blood in urine
Ketouria	Ketones present
Proteinuria	Protein present
Pyuria	Leucocytes present (e.g. infection)

Microbiology

Samples of body fluids including blood, sputum, urine, cerebrospinal fluid (CSF), wound swabs, and swabs from mucosal surfaces are sent to the microbiology department for culture and sensitivities.

The results indicate the organisms that have been identified and the antibiotics to which the organisms are sensitive. Usually the cultures (the identified organisms) are reported first, with the sensitivities reported a few days later. The initial choice of antibiotic therapy is informed by the clinical signs the patient is exhibiting and local antibiotic policies. This therapy can then be tailored when the cultures become available and refined further when sensitivities are reported.

The antibiotics listed on the report are not listed in order of sensitivity, although this is a common misconception.

Choice of antibiotic

In both empirical prescribing and prescribing with knowledge of bacterial sensitivities, the choice of antibiotic depends on both patient and drug factors. Patient factors include: the site of infection, severity of infection, age of the patient, renal or hepatic impairment, immune status, pregnancy or breast feeding, route of administration, drug allergies. Drug factors include: efficacy, safety, the need for therapeutic drug monitoring, availability in the required pharmaceutical form and cost.

Section 5
Medical abbreviations

The use of medical abbreviations whilst taking patient notes is discouraged. The reason for this is obvious – the possibility of confusion and error – particularly in cases where there is more than one meaning for an abbreviation.

However, many of the abbreviations are standard and clearly understood in context. These standard abbreviations are listed below.

A

A&E	Accident and Emergency department
A&O	alert and orientated
A&W	alive and well
AAA	abdominal aortic aneurysm
Ab	abdomen, antibody
Ab	antibody
AB	abortion
ABG	arterial blood gas
ABPM	ambulatory blood pressure monitoring
ABW	actual body weight
Abx	antibiotics
ACS	acute coronary syndrome
ADH	antidiuretic hormone
ADLs	activities of daily living
ADR	adverse drug reaction
AF	atrial fibrillation, atrial flutter
AFB	acid fast bacillus (mycobacteria)
AFP	alpha foetoprotein
AIDS	acquired immune deficiency syndrome

AI/AR	aortic insufficiency/aortic regurgitation
AKA	above knee amputation
AKI	acute kidney injury
ALD	alcoholic liver disease
Alk. phos	alkaline phosphatase
ALL	acute lymphoblastic leukaemia
ALT	alanine aminotransferase
AMI	acute myocardial infarction, anterior myocardial infarction
AML	acute myeloid leukaemia
ANA	antinuclear antibody
ANF	antinuclear factor, atrial natriuretic factor
APTT	activated partial thromboplastin time
ARDS	acute respiratory distress syndrome
AS	aortic stenosis, atherosclerosis, ankylosing spondylitis
AST	aspartate transaminase
AV	aortic value, arteriovenous, atrioventricular
AXR	abdominal X-ray

B

BBB	blood brain barrier
BE	barium enema
BKA	below knee amputation
BM	bone marrow, bowel movement
BMI	body mass index
BMR	basal metabolic rate
BMs	blood glucose level
BNO	bowels not open
BNP	brain natriuretic peptide
BO	bowels open
BOR	bowels open regularly
BP	blood pressure
BPH	benign prostatic hypertrophy
BPM	beats per minute
BS	breath sounds, bowel sounds
BSA	body surface area
BUN	blood urea nitrogen
Bx	biopsy

C

Ca, CA	cancer, carcinoma
CABG	coronary artery bypass graft
CAD	coronary artery disease
CAPD	continuous ambulatory peritoneal dialysis
CAT	computerised axial tomography
CCF	congestive cardiac failure
CCU	coronary care unit, critical care unit
CDT	Clostridium difficile toxin
CF	cystic fibrosis
CHD	coronary heart disease
CHF	congestive heart failure
CK	creatinine kinase
CKD	chronic kidney disease
CLL	chronic lymphocytic leukaemia
CML	chronic myeloid leukaemia
CMV	cytomegalovirus
CNS	central nervous system
CO	cardiac output
C/O	complains of
COAD	chronic obstructive airways disease
COC	combined oral contraceptive
COPD	chronic obstructive pulmonary disease
CPK	creatinine phosphokinase
CPR	cardiopulmonary resuscitation
Cr	creatinine
CrCl	creatinine clearance
CRP	C-reactive protein
CSF	cerebrospinal fluid
CSU	catheter specimen of urine
CT	computed tomography
cTnI	cardiac troponin I
cTnT	cardiac troponin T
CTPA	computerised tomography pulmonary angiogram
CVA	cerebrovascular accident
CVP	central venous pressure
CVS	cardiovascular system

CXR	chest X-ray
Cy	cyanosis

D

Δ	diagnosis
ΔΔ	differential diagnosis
D	deceased
D&C	dilatation and curettage (uterine 'scrape')
DD	differential diagnosis
D&V	diarrhoea and vomiting
DH	drug history
DHS	dynamic hip screw
DHx	drug history
DIC	disseminated intravascular coagulation
DKA	diabetic ketoacidosis
DM	diabetes mellitus
DMARD	disease-modifying anti-rheumatic drug
DNA	did not attend (outpatient appointments)
DNR	do not resuscitate
DOA	dead on arrival
DOB	date of birth
DTP	diphtheria, tetanus, pertussis
DTs	delirium tremens
DU	duodenal ulcer
DVT	deep vein thrombosis
Dx	diagnosis
DXT	radiotherapy

E

ECF	extracellular fluid
ECG	electrocardiogram
ECT	electroconvulsive therapy
EEG	electroencephalogram
EHC	emergency hormonal contraception
ENT	ears, nose and throat
ERCP	endoscopic retrograde cholangiopancreatography
ESBL	extended spectrum beta lactamase
ESR	erythrocyte sedimentation rate

ESRF	end stage renal failure
ET	endotracheal
EtOH	alcohol (ethanol)
EUA	examination under anaesthetic

F

#	fracture
F&W	fit and well
FB	foreign body, finger breadths
FBC	full blood count
FBS	fasting blood sugar
FEVI	forced expiratory volume in 1 second
FFP	fresh frozen plasma
FH	family history
FHR	foetal heart rate
FOB	faecal occult blood
FRC	functional residual capacity
FTT	failure to thrive
FU	follow up
FUO	fever of unknown origin
FVC	forced vital capacity
FY1 or F1	foundation year 1 doctor
FY2 or F2	foundation year 2 doctor

G

G	gravida (pregnancy), e.g. G4 = 4th pregnancy
GA	general anaesthetic
GB	gall bladder
GCS	Glasgow Coma Scale
GFR	glomerular filtration rate
GGT	gamma glutamyl transferase
GIT	gastrointestinal tract
GORD	gastro-oesophageal reflux disease
GP	General Practitioner
Grav	gravida (pregnancy)
GTT	glucose tolerance test
GU	genitourinary, gastric ulcer
GUM	genitourinary medicine

H

H&L	heart and lungs
Hb	haemoglobin
HbAlc	glycosylated haemoglobin
HBPM	home blood pressure monitoring
Hct	haematocrit
HCG	human chorionic gonadotrophin
HDL	high density lipoprotein
HDU	high dependency unit
HIV	human immunodeficiency virus
H/O	history of
HPC	history of presenting complaint
HPI	history of presenting illness
HR	heart rate
HS	heart sounds
HSS	hyperosmolar hyperglycaemic state
HSV	herpes simplex virus
HTN	hypertension
Hx	history

I

IBD	inflammatory bowel disease
IBS	irritable bowel syndrome
IBW	ideal body weight
ICF	intracellular fluid
ICS	intercostal space
ICU	intensive care unit
ID	intradermal, infectious disease
IDDM	insulin dependent diabetes mellitus
Ig	immunoglobulin
IHD	ischaemic heart disease
IM	intramuscular
IMP	impression
INR	international normalised ratio
IP	intraperitoneal, intrapleural, inpatient
IPPB	intermittent positive pressure breathing
IT	intrathecal

ITP	idiopathic thrombocytopenia
ITU	intensive therapy unit (same as ICU)
IUD	intrauterine device
IV	intravenous
Ix	investigations

J

JACCOL	jaundice, clubbing, cyanosis, oedema & lymphadenopathy
JVP	jugular venous pressure

L

LAD	lymphadenopathy
LBBB	left bundle branch block
LBO	large bowel obstruction
LDH	lactate dehydrogenase
LFA	low friction arthroplasty
LFTs	liver function tests
LIF	left iliac fossa
LIH	left inguinal hernia
LMP	last menstrual period
LMS	locomotor system
LMWH	low molecular weight heparin
LN	lymph node
LOC	loss of consciousness
LP	lumbar puncture
LRTI	lower respiratory tract infection
LUQ	left upper quadrant
LVF	left ventricular failure
LVH	left ventricular hypertrophy

M

MAO	monoamine oxidase
MCH	mean corpuscular haemoglobin
MCHC	mean corpuscular haemoglobin concentration
MC&S	microscopy, culture and sensitivity
MCV	mean corpuscular volume
MG	myasthenia gravis
MI	myocardial infarction, mitral incompetence/insufficiency
MIC	minimum inhibitory concentration

ML	midline
MM	multiple myeloma
MMR	measles, mumps and rubella vaccination
MRCP	magnetic resonance cholangiopancreatography
MRI	magnetic resonance imaging
MRSA	methicillin resistant Staphylococcus aureus
MS	multiple sclerosis, mitral stenosis
MSE	mental state examination
MSU	midstream urine specimen

N

N	normal
N&T	nose and throat
N&V	nausea and vomiting
NAD	nothing abnormal detected
NBM	nil by mouth
NFR	not for resuscitation
NG	nasogastric
NHL	non-Hodgkin's lymphoma
NIDDM	non-insulin dependent diabetes mellitus
NIPPV	non-invasive positive pressure ventilation
NoF	neck of femur
N/S	normal saline
NSTEMI	non-ST elevated myocardial infarction
NSU	non-specific urethritis

O

°	absent (e.g. °clubbing = no clubbing present)
O	oedema
OA	osteoarthritis
O/A	on admission
OCP	oral contraceptive pill
OD	overdose
O/E	on examination
OGD	oesophagogastroduodenoscopy
OOB	out of bed
OP	outpatient
OPD	outpatient department

OT	occupational therapy

P

P	pulse
P&A	percussion and auscultation
PA	pernicious anaemia
PAC	premature atrial contraction
PAT	paroxysmal atrial tachycardia
PC	presenting complaint
PCOS	polycystic ovary syndrome
PCP	pneumocystis jirovecii pneumonia
pCO_2	partial pressure of carbon dioxide
PCV	packed cell volume
PD	peritoneal dialysis
PE	pulmonary embolism
PEFR	peak expiratory flow rate
PEG	percutaneous endoscopic gastrostomy
PERLA	pupils equal and reactive to light and accommodation
PERLAC	pupils equally reacting to light, accommodation consensual
PFR	peak flow rate
PID	pelvic inflammatory disease
PKD	polycystic kidney disease
PKU	phenylketonuria
PM	post mortem
PMH	past medical history
PN	percussion note
PND	paroxysmal nocturnal dyspnoea
pO_2	partial pressure of oxygen
POP	progesterone only pill, plaster of Paris
PR	per rectum
PSH	past surgical history
PTCA	percutaneous transluminal coronary angioplasty
PTSD	post-traumatic stress disorder
PT	prothrombin time
PTT	partial thromboplastin time
PTWR	post-take ward round
PU	passed urine, peptic ulcer
PUD	peptic ulcer disease

PUO	pyrexia of unknown origin
PV	per vaginam (through the vagina)
PVD	peripheral vascular disease

Q

QOL	quality of life

R

RA	rheumatoid arthritis
RBBB	right bundle branch block
RBC	red blood cells
RDA	recommended daily amount
RDS	respiratory distress syndrome
REM	rapid eye movement
RF	rheumatoid factor
RIF	right iliac fossa
RIH	right inguinal hernia
ROM	range of movement
ROS	review of systems, review of symptoms
RR	respiratory rate, rate and rhythm (pulse)
RRT	renal replacement therapy
RS	respiratory system
RSI	repetitive strain injury
RT	radiotherapy
RTC	road traffic collision, return to clinic (for outpatient appointment)
RUQ	right upper quadrant
RVF	right ventricular failure
RVH	right ventricular hypertrophy
Rx	treatment/prescription

S

S1	first heart sound
S2	second heart sound
S3	third heart sound
S4	fourth heart sound
SB	seen by, small bowel
SBE	subacute bacterial endocarditis
SBO	small bowel obstruction
SC	subcutaneous

SH	social history
SIADH	syndrome of inappropriate ADH secretion
SLE	systemic lupus erythematosus
SOB	shortness of breath
SOBE	shortness of breath on exertion
SOL	space occupying lesion
SR	sinus rhythm, slow release
STI	sexually transmitted infection
STI–8	specialist trainee year 1–8 doctor
STD	sexually transmitted disease
STEMI	ST-elevated myocardial infarction
SVT	supraventricular tachycardia
Sx	symptoms

T

T°	temperature
T3	tri-iodothyronine
T4	thyroxine
T&C	type and cross-match (blood)
TATT	tired all the time
TB	tuberculosis
TCI	to come in (admit to hospital)
TFTs	thyroid function tests
THR	total hip replacement
TIA	transient ischaemic attack
TKR	total knee replacement
TLC	total lung capacity
TOP	termination of pregnancy
TPN	total parenteral nutrition
TPR	temperature, pulse, respiratory rate
TRH	thyrotropin releasing hormone
TSH	thyroid stimulating hormone
TTA	to take away (discharge medication)
TTH	to take home (discharge medication)
TTO	to take out (discharge medication)
TURP	transurethral resection of the prostate
TWOC	trial without catheter
Tx	treatment, transplant, transfusion (blood)

U

U&Es	urea and electrolytes
UC	ulcerative colitis, urinary catheter
UFH	unfractionated heparin
ULN	upper limit of normal
UO	urine output
URTI	upper respiratory tract infection
US	ultrasound, urinary system
USS	ultrasound scan
UTI	urinary tract infection

V

VC	vital capacity
VF	ventricular fibrillation
VO	verbal order
VQ	lung ventilation/perfusion scan
VRE	vancomycin resistant enterococci
VS	vital signs
VT	ventricular tachycardia
VZV	varicella zoster virus

W

WBC	white blood cells, white blood count
WBS	whole body scan
WCC	white cell count
WNL	within normal limits
WPW	Wolff-Parkinson-White Syndrome
WR	ward round

X

XM	X match (cross match)

Index